Guitar Chords in Context

Construction and Application

Published by www.fundamental-changes.com

ISBN: 978-1503152670

www.fundamental-changes.com

Also By Joseph Alexander

Fundamental Changes in Jazz Guitar I: The Major ii V I for Bebop Guitar

Minor ii V Mastery for Jazz Guitar

Jazz Blues Soloing for Guitar

Guitar Scales in Context

Drop 2 Chord Voicings for Jazz and Modern Guitar

The CAGED System and 100 Licks for Blues Guitar

The Complete Guide to Playing Blues Guitar Book One: Rhythm Guitar

The Complete Guide to Playing Blues Guitar Book Two: Melodic Phrasing

The Complete Guide to Playing Blues Guitar Book Three: Beyond Pentatonics

The Complete Guide to Playing Blues Guitar Compilation (Paperback)

The Complete Technique, Theory and Scales Compilation for Guitar (Paperback)

Sight Reading Mastery for Guitar

Complete Technique for Modern Guitar

Rock Guitar Un-CAGED: The CAGED System and 100 Licks for Rock Guitar

**Audio recorded by Pete Sklaroff and Available From
www.fundamental-changes.com/audio-downloads.**

Index

Introduction to Part One

In over twenty five years as a guitarist, I have come across many different chord dictionaries that profess to show you *every* possible chord that is playable on the guitar. Some of these are massive tomes that probably do exactly what they promise, although I have always found most of them extremely unusable.

These chord dictionaries may be well organised and comprehensively researched, but I have always found that without showing some sort of practical application in which to use the chord they have always been of limited benefit.

After a few such experiences, I realised that instead of reaching for a chord book, the best possible use of my time was to learn how chords were constructed and named and how the guitar neck functioned in terms of note and interval location.

By learning how a chord was constructed, where it came from, and how it functioned, and armed with the fretboard knowledge to be able to see where the notes/intervals actually were on the guitar, I quickly realised that I would never need a chord dictionary again.

I can now construct any chord I want instantly because I see the guitar neck in terms of intervals.
Another limitation of traditional chord dictionaries is that they do not generally show how to use a chord in any sort of context. It's all very well to know *how* to play a m(Maj7) in four inversions, but if you don't know *when* to play it this information is somewhat redundant.

In this book I have tried to give realistic musical examples and some sort of context for each of the chords discussed. The majority of chords come up fairly regularly and you will often see them in rhythm charts, especially if you are playing jazz or fusion. There are a few chords at the end of the book that crop up occasionally and are far less common. Part One of this series is organised in terms of usefulness!

One final limitation I have found with traditional chord dictionaries is a lack of aural examples. If you're learning a chord you should be able to *hear* that you're playing it correctly. To help with this I have included over one hundred audio examples that you can download for free from **www.fundamental-changes.com/audio-downloads**. You can hear every chord played in at least three different voicings and every example chord progression is also recorded to help you musically understand the function of each example.

This series of chord books is split into three parts.

Part One is designed to give you an immediate, practical understanding of how all of the basic chord forms are constructed, played and used. Each chord is thoroughly discussed, analysed and built from first principles. Every chord is given with a root on the 6th, 5th and 4th strings so you will always have a convenient fingering to reach for, wherever you are on the guitar neck. Part One is about understanding, hearing and applying the essential concepts of chord construction. Some basic common substitutions are introduced when appropriate, either to help us reach extensions, or to vastly simplify a complex chord structure.

The prerequisite to Part One is the ability to play the basic 'open' position chords, such as D, G and C etc. It will also be very helpful if you are comfortable with barre chords and the locations of the notes on the bottom three strings of the guitar.

Part Two focuses on specific chord structures, their inversions, voicings and voice leading. It covers 'drop 2', 'drop 3' and 'drop 2 and 4' chords on all string groups. Any '7th' chord can be played in four different inversions: with either the root, 3rd, 5th or 7th in the bass. These concepts allow a lot of voicing possibilities and hundreds of wonderful musical opportunities. It sounds like a lot of work, but even with just a few 'drop 2' voicings you will quickly add massive depth to your rhythm guitar playing and quickly find that your vision of the guitar neck increases dramatically.

Each concept is taught in a tangible, well-paced, musical way and throughout the book there are hundreds of examples to make sure you're learning every chord in a cohesive way. The idea is to build chord 'licks' around common sequences to contextualise and internalise useful musical statements. *(Available December 2014.)*

Part Three studies chord melody and walking basslines built around the voicings learnt in parts one and two. Building from these first principles and learning how to use extensions and specific structures to highlight the melody notes that matter, Part Three of Guitar Chords in Context teaches you all the tools you need to really advance your chord melody playing. *(Available in 2015.)*

In Part One, you may find that things start to get 'jazzy' as we progress through the differing chord types. This is because the majority of the more complex chords we play as musicians are often found in this genre. They are very occasionally used in rock music, but this would be the exception rather than the norm. If jazz is not for you, then don't despair! The knowledge gained by working through this book, both in terms of chord vocabulary and fretboard freedom will greatly benefit you, whatever your musical interests.

Don't forget that you get all the audio examples in this book free from
www.fundamental-changes.com/audio-downloads.

Have fun!

Joseph.

Chapter One: Basic Theory, Chord Types and Construction

A chord is defined as any group of three or more notes played together. They are normally formed by stacking notes on top of each other from a particular scale. Most of the chords in this book are formed from *harmonising* the major scale.

To form a chord, we simply stack alternate notes from a scale. For example, in the scale of C Major:
C D E F G A B C

We take the first, third and fifth notes (C E and G), and play them together to form a C Major chord.

(C) D (E) F (G) A B C

Example 1a:

If you notice, we took the *first* note C, then skipped the next note (D) and landed on the *third* note E. We repeated this process and skipped the fourth note (F) and landed on the *fifth* note G. The notes played together in this way are called a *triad*.

The first, third and fifth notes of a major scale form a major chord. This is true of any major scale. This chord is given the formula 1 3 5.

The formula 1 3 5 gives us the notes C E and G, however, we can alter any of the notes to form a different type of chord. For example, if we *flatten* the third we generate the formula 1 b3 5. Using the root note of C again, we now have the notes C *Eb* G.

Example 1b:

As you can hear, this structure has a very different sound from the previous major chord.

Any chord with the structure 1 b3 5 is a minor chord. In fact, *any* chord that contains a b3 is defined as a minor sound.

We can also flatten the 5th of the chord. The structure 1 3 b5 is not very common in music although it does sometimes occur in jazz. However, the structure 1 b3 b5 occurs frequently. It is called a *diminished* or occasionally a *minor b5* chord.

The formula 1 b3 b5 built on a root of C generates the notes C Eb Gb.

Example 1c:

This is a bit of a stretch to play on the guitar, but the notes do not have to be played in this order. They can be played more comfortably like this:

Example 1d:

To achieve this voicing I moved the b3 of the chord up by one octave.

As you can hear, the diminished chord has a dark and sinister air to it.

The three triads you have learned so far are

1 3 5 Major
1 b3 5 Minor
1 b3 b5 Diminished or just 'Dim'
Most chords you come across in music, no matter how complicated can normally be categorised into one of these basic types. Jazz chord progressions however are normally formed from richer sounding '7th chords' which are the focus of this book.

There is, however, one more permutation that crops up occasionally, it is the augmented triad, 1 3 #5.

From a root note of C, the notes generated by this formula are C E G#. There are two tones between each of the notes of the chord.

Example 1e:

Two useful voicings of the augmented (Aug) triad are

Example 1f:

Finally, there are two types of triad that do *not* include a 3rd. These chords are normally named 'suspended' (or just 'sus' chords), as the lack of the 3rd gives an unresolved feel to their character.

In a 'sus' 2 chord the 3rd is replaced with the 2nd of the scale, and in a sus4 chord, the 3rd is replaced with the 4th of the scale.

In C, the notes generated by the formula 1 2 5 are C D and G

Example 1g

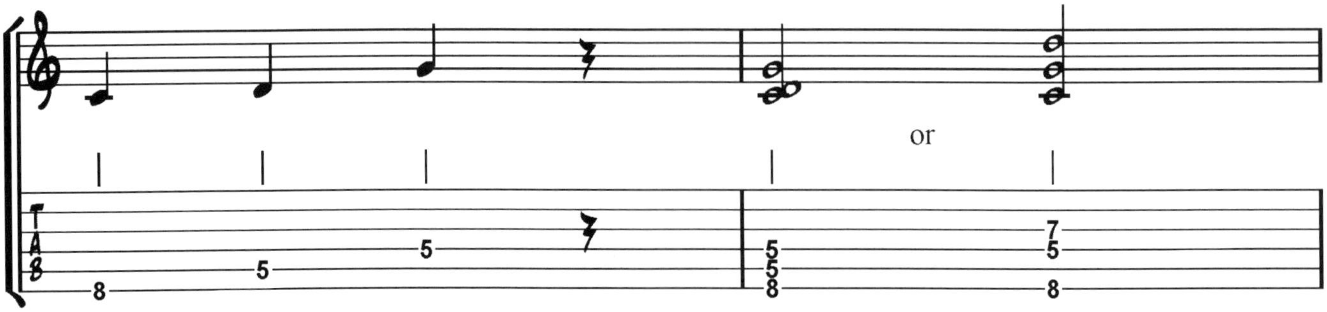

The notes generated by the formula 1 4 5 are C F and G.

Example 1h

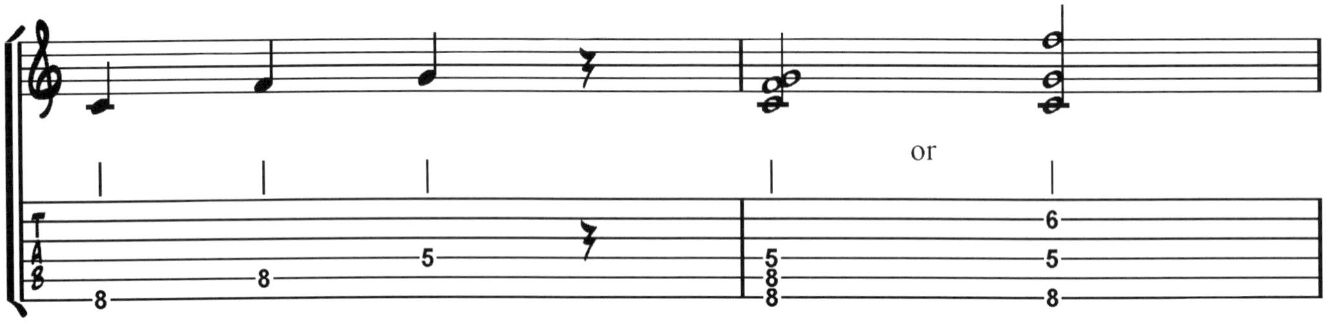

It is first important that you learn to play some useful chord voicings of these basic triads as they do sometimes occur in jazz chord charts, especially in early 'swing' jazz.

In any chord, it is acceptable to *double* any note. For example, a major chord could contain two roots, two 5ths and only one 3rd. There were rules to govern their use in 'classical' times, although these days there are common chord shapes or 'grips' on the guitar that are frequently used.

As the focus of this book is on 7th chords, which are more common in jazz, only a few of the basic triad chord shapes are shown here.

Major Chord Shapes:

Example 1i:

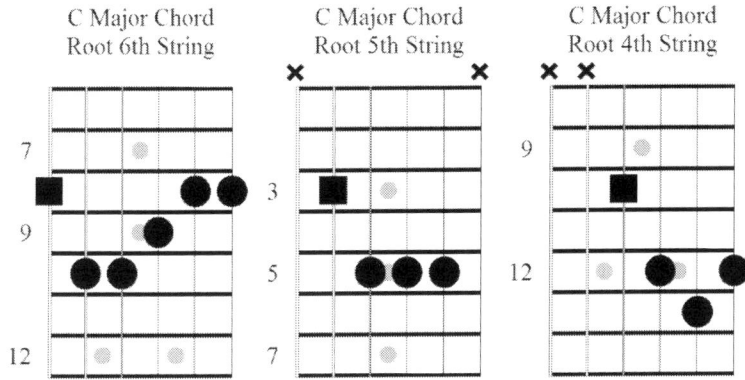

Minor Chord Shapes:

Example 1j:

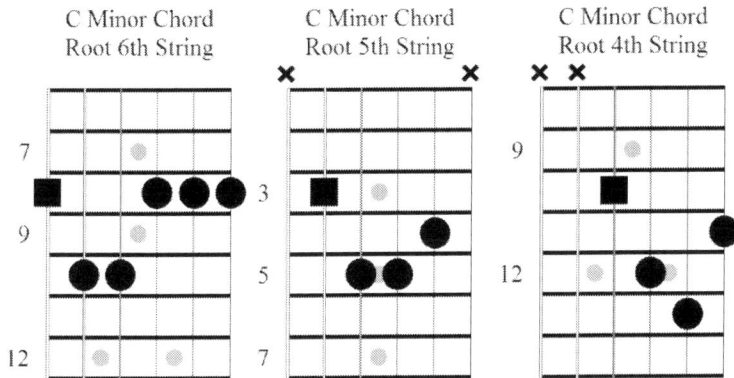

Diminished (minor b5) Chord Shapes:

Example 1k:

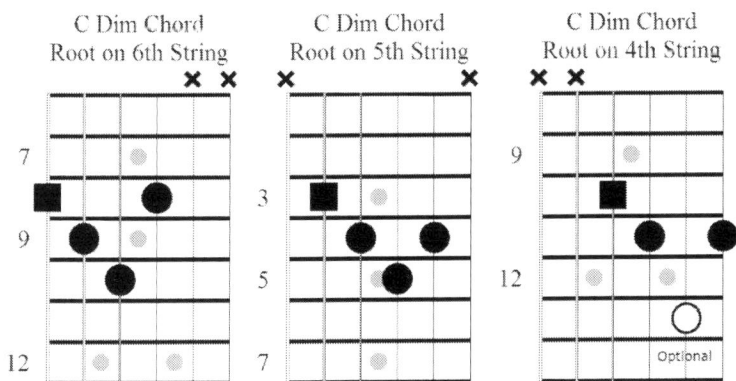

Augmented (major #5) Chord Shapes:

Example 1l:

C Aug Chord
Root on 6th String

C Aug Chord
Root on 5th String

C Aug Chord
Root on 4th String

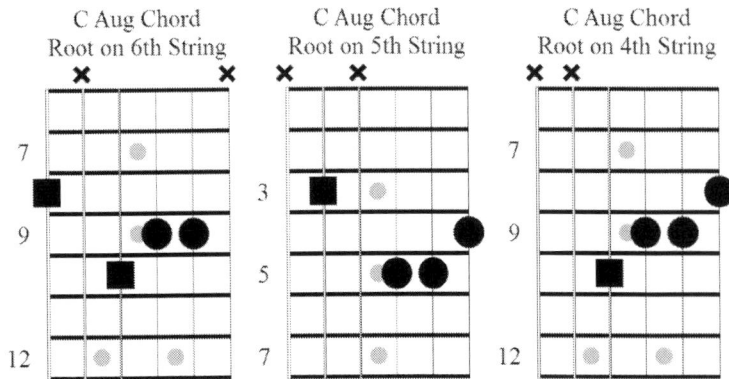

Suspended 2nd Chord Shapes:

Example 1m:

C Sus2 Chord
Root on 6th String

C Sus2 Chord
Root on 5th String

C Sus2 Chord
Root on 4th String

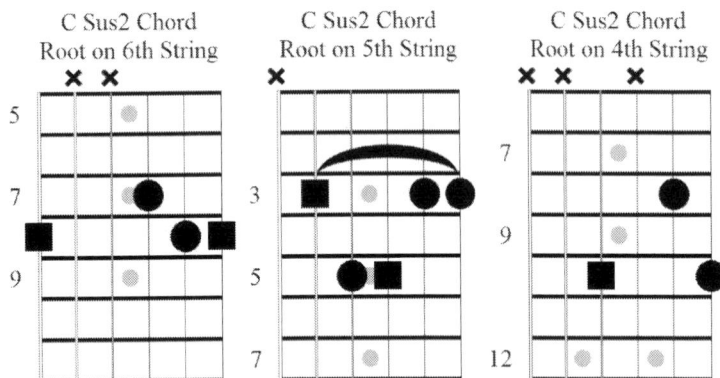

Suspended 4th Chord Shapes:

Example 1n:

C Sus4 Chord
Root on 6th String

C Sus4 Chord
Root on 5th String

C Sus4 Chord
Root on 4th String

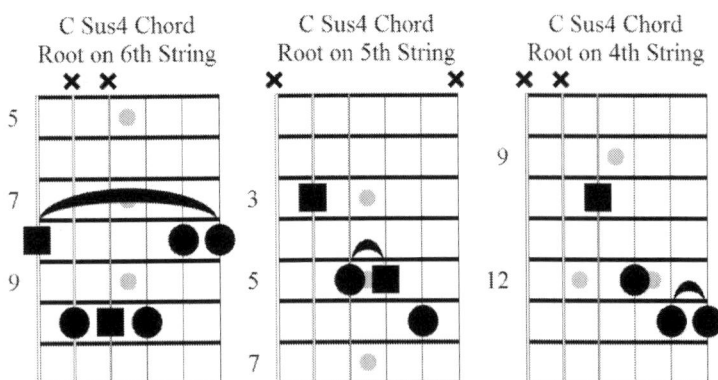

You probably already know most of these shapes, but if you don't, my advice is to ignore them for now while we get focused on 7th chords. You can come back to these voicings as a reference when you need them.

To create a major 7th chord we simply extend the '1 3 5' formula by an extra note so it becomes '1 3 5 7'.

Instead of C E G we now have C E G B:

(C) D (E) F (G) A (B)

Example 1o:

In these voicings, I have changed the order of the notes to make the chord playable on the guitar. The chord is now voiced 1 5 7 3.

As the major 7th's chord formula is 1 3 5 7, you might expect that the minor 7th's formula would be 1 b3 5 7. This, however, is not the case.

To create a minor 7 chord we add a *b7* to a minor triad. The formula is 1 b3 5 *b7*.

The formula 1 b3 5 b7 built on a root note of C generates the notes C Eb G Bb.

Example 1p:

Once again, the notes in the lower chord voicing have been rearranged to make the voicing playable on the guitar.

As you're probably wondering, a minor triad with a *natural 7* on the top 1 b3 5 **7** is called a *"minor major 7th"* or m(Maj7) chord and we will discuss these structures in chapter twelve as they are an important sound in jazz. They are given this name because they are minor triads with a *major* 7th added on top.

When we extend a minor b5 chord to become a 7th chord, we once again add a *b7*, not a natural 7. In fact, it is a general rule that if a triad has a b3, it is more common to add a b7 to form a four-note '7th' chord.

As you can see in the previous paragraph, this is not always the case, so be careful when applying that 'rule'.

A (diminished) minor b5 chord with an added b7 has the formula 1 b3 b5 b7 and generates the notes C Eb Gb Bb when built from the root note of C. This chord is named 'Minor 7 flat 5' or m7b5 for short. It also is common for m7b5 chords to be referred to as 'half diminished' chords.

Example 1q:

Finally, we come to one of the most common chords in jazz; the dominant 7 chord. It is formed by adding a b7 to a major triad. 1 3 5 b7. With a root of C this formula generates the notes C E G Bb.

Because of the fundamental major triad 1 3 5, this chord is a 'major' type chord, but the added b7 gives it an extra bit of tension.

Example 1r:

These four chord types can be summarised:

Chord Type	Formula	Short Name
Major 7	1 3 5 7	'maj7'
Dominant 7	1 3 5 b7	'7'
Minor 7	1 b3 5 b7	'm7'
Minor 7 b5	1 b3 b5 b7	'm7b5'

It is the modern way of thinking that *all* chord types in jazz function in one of the above contexts. We will discuss this at length later, although what this means in simple terms is that even a complex chord, such as C7#5b9, can be viewed in its simplest form as just C7.

A C Minor 11 chord can be simplified to become a Cm7-type chord and a C major 9th chord can be reduced to a Cmaj7-type chord. This is very useful when viewing jazz tunes from a soloing perspective. There are a few exceptions to these rules when playing chords, and those will be addressed individually.

This idea of chord 'types' or families is especially useful when we're starting out playing jazz chords, or when we're given a particularly difficult chord chart to read with little preparation time.

Chapter Two: Basic Common Chord Voicings

Now that we understand how the most common chords are constructed, we can begin to learn some useful voicings. The voicings in this chapter are designed to 'get you through the tune'. They are the first jazz chord voicings that most guitarists learn, and will remain a part of your vocabulary from this point forward.

We will begin by learning three voicings of each of the fundamental chord types, maj7, 7, m7, and m7b5 and we will apply them to a common jazz chord progression that uses these chord types. It is important at this point that you know where the notes are on your guitar fretboard as we are now learning 'movable' barre chord forms of each chord.

For example, we will learn a barre chord '7' shape and if you want to play this chord as a C7 you will need to place it so that the root note is C. If you wish to play it as an F7 you will have to move it so that the root note is F. In order to do this you should at least be familiar with the notes on the bottom three strings:

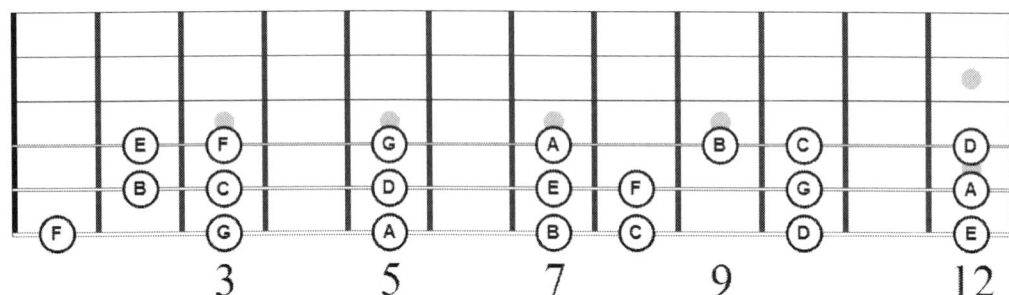

We are going to learn to play the following chord progression using three different jazz chord voicings.

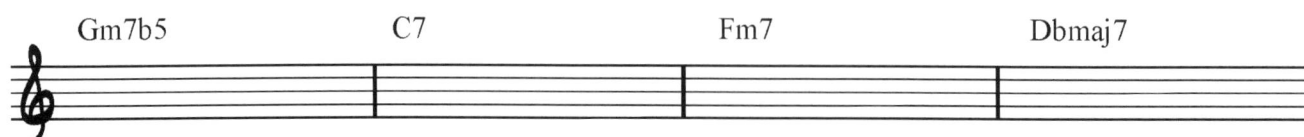

As you can see, this chord progression uses each of the chord types from the previous chapter once.

Let's begin by learning voicings of these chords that have their root on the 6th string. The numbers written on the notes are suggested fingerings. If you find it easier to use different fingers then please feel free to use them.

You may find it easier to play the Fm7 chord 'up an octave' at the 13th fret, this is also fine.

Gm7b5 Chord
Root 6th String

C7 Chord
Root 6th String

Fm7 Chord
Root 6th String

Db Maj7 Chord
Root 6th String

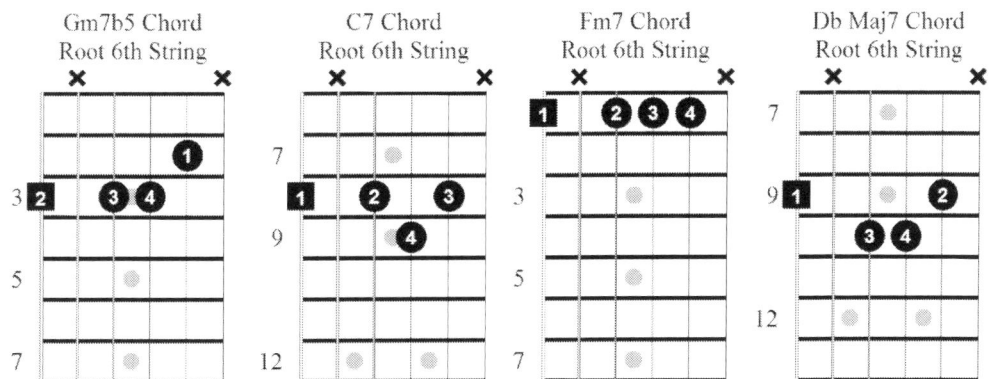

Spend time learning these chords and gradually join them together until you can play **example 2a:**

| Gm7b5 | C7 | Fm7 | Fm7 | Dbmaj7 |

or

```
Gm7b5   C7    Fm7   Fm7    Dbmaj7
  2      8     1     13      9
  3      9     1     13     10
  3      8     1     13     10
  3      8     1     13      9
```

You will notice that when using these chord voicings your hand is moving around a great deal on the fretboard. Don't worry about this for now as when you have a few more voicings under your fingers you can start to smooth out the movements.

Next, learn the same common chords voiced with the root on the 5th string:

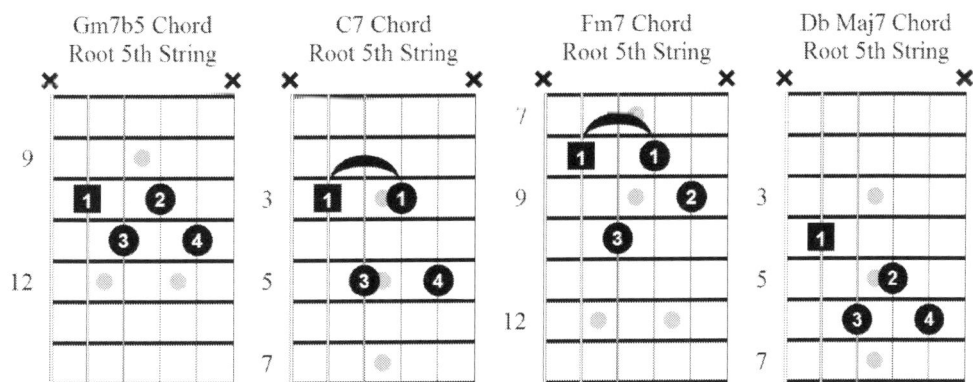

Gm7b5 Chord
Root 5th String

C7 Chord
Root 5th String

Fm7 Chord
Root 5th String

Db Maj7 Chord
Root 5th String

Again, work towards playing the same chord sequence using just the 5th string voicings:

Example 2b:

Before moving on to learning these chord types with a 4th string root, try combining the 6th and 5th string chords to voice the chords closer together.

Try beginning on a 6th string for the Gm7b5 chord and then move to the closest voicing of the C7 chord when you change. Always look for the closest possible voicing when you change chords. One way of doing this could be:

Example 2c:

Another way to practice this is to begin on the 5th string voicing of the Gm7b5 chord and repeat the same process.

Example 2d:

Gm7b5 Chord — Root 5th String | C7 Chord — Root 6th String | Fm7 Chord — Root 5th String | Db Maj7 Chord — Root 6th String

Gm7b5   C7   Fm7   Dbmaj7

By changing strings in this way we can always create smoother *'voice leading'* between each of the chords in the chord progression. (Voice leading is the technique of arranging chords so that each note moves the smallest possible distance during each chord change). It is also easier to play these chords at speed because our hand is not moving such great distances.

Now let's look at these common chords played with a 4th string root.

Gm7b5 Chord — Root 4th String | C7 Chord — Root 4th String | Fm7 Chord — Root 4th String | Db Maj7 Chord — Root 4th String

Try playing the same chord sequence just using these chords. This example may be a little more difficult as many people are not as familiar with the note names on the 4th string as they are with the 5th and 6th strings. Take your time and persevere.

Example 2e:

Gm7b5   C7   Fm7   Dbmaj7

As before, these chords jump up and down the neck a lot, so we can combine them with 5th string chords to make them flow more easily.

Try beginning the chord sequence on a 5th string Gm7b5 and then move to a 4th string C7.

Example 2f:

Gm7b5 Chord
Root 5th String

C7 Chord
Root 4th String

Fm7 Chord
Root 5th String

Db Maj7 Chord
Root 4th String

Gm7b5   C7   Fm7   Dbmaj7

We could also change the chord voicing we use for the final Dbmaj7 in this sequence. If we play it as a 6th string root chord, the voicings will flow together more smoothly:

Example 2g:

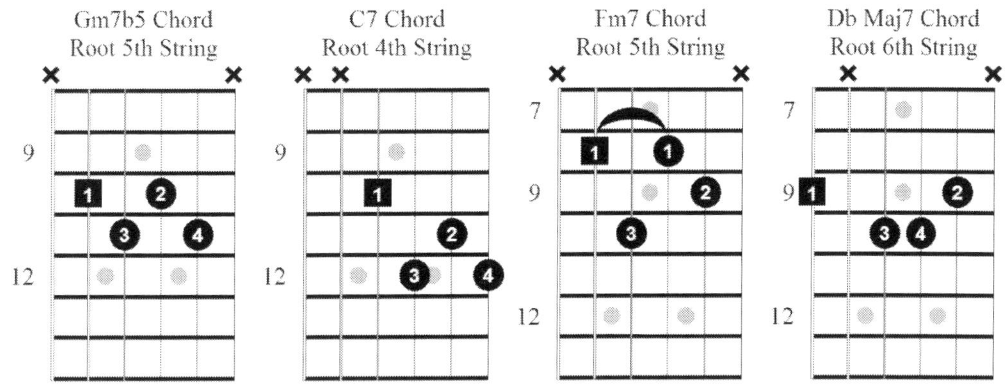

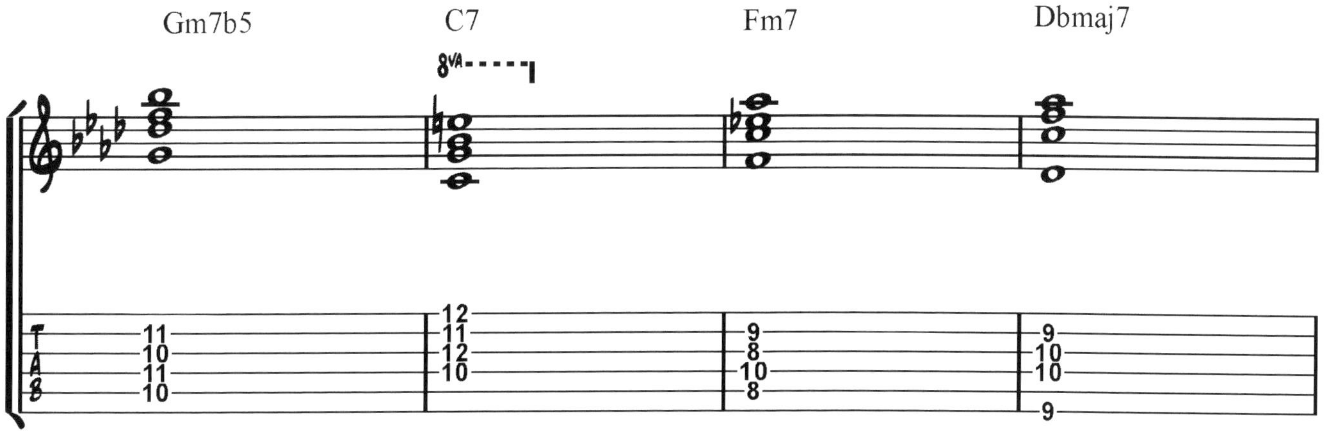

Try starting the chord sequence on different strings and see how closely you can voice-lead the chord progression. Here is just one possible 'route' through the changes starting on the 6th string:

Example 2h:

Gm7b5 Chord
Root 6th String

C7 Chord
Root 5th String

Fm7 Chord
Root 4th String

Db Maj7 Chord
Root 5th String

Gm7b5   C7   Fm7   Dbmaj7

Try finding ways through the following two chord progressions using the voicings discussed in this chapter:

1)

Dm7   G7   CMaj7   Dbm7b5

2)

Cm7   Em7b5   BbMaj7   G7

Begin by playing through each progression using chords all with roots on the same string, then combine the 6th and 5th string voicings. Next combine the 4th and 5th string voicings and finally find the closest chord voicings using roots on all three strings.

Chapter Three: Diatonic Extensions to Dominant 7 Chords

In jazz, it is common to add diatonic 'extensions' and chromatic 'alterations' to dominant 7 chords. A natural or 'diatonic' extension is a note that is added to the basic 1 3 5 b7 chord, but lies within the original parent scale of the dominant chord. In other words, to form an extended dominant chord we continue skipping notes in the scale, just as we did when we originally learnt to form a chord.

We can extend the basic 1 3 5 b7 chord formula to include the 9th, 11th and 13th scale tones.

These extensions occur when we extend a scale beyond the first octave. For example, here is the parent scale of a C7 chord (C Mixolydian):

C	D	E	F	G	A	Bb	C	D	E	F	G	A	Bb	C
1	2	3	4	5	6	b7	1/8	9	3	11	5	13	b7	1

Notice that in the second octave, if a note is included in the original chord it is still referred to as 1, 3, 5, or b7. This is because the function of these notes never changes in the chord: A 3rd will always define whether a chord is major or minor and the b7 will always be an essential part of a m7 or 7 chord.

The notes *between* the chord tones are the notes that have changed their names. Instead of 2, 4 and 6, they are now 9, 11, and 13. These are called *compound* intervals

In very simple terms you could say that a C13 chord could contain *all* the intervals up until the 13th:

1 3 5 b7 9 11 and 13 – C E G Bb D F and A

In practice though, this is a huge amount of notes (we only have six strings), and playing that many notes at the same time produces an extremely heavy, undesirable sound because many of the notes will clash with one another.

The answer to this problem is to remove some of the notes from the chord, but how do we know which ones?

There are no set rules about which notes to leave out in an extended chord, however there *are* some guidelines about how to define a chord sound and what *does* need to be included.

To define a chord as major or minor, you must include some kind of 3rd.

To define a chord as dominant 7, major 7 or minor 7, you must include some kind of 7th.

These notes, the 3rds and 7ths are called guide tones, and they are the most essential notes in any chord. It may surprise you, but these notes are more important than even the root of the chord and quite often in jazz rhythm guitar playing, the root of the chord is dropped entirely.

We will look more closely at guide tone or 'shell' chord voicings in the next chapter, but for now we will examine common ways to play the extensions that regularly occur on dominant chords in jazz progressions.

To name a dominant chord, we always look to the highest extension that is included, so if the notes were 1, 3, b7 and 13 we would call this a dominant 13, or just '13' chord. Notice that it doesn't include the 5th, the 9th or the 11th but it is still called a '13' chord.

As long as we have the 3rd and b7th a chord will always be a dominant voicing.

We will begin by looking at a fairly common voicing of a D7 chord. In the following example, each *interval* of the chord is labelled in the diagram.

In D7 the intervals 1 3 5 b7 are the notes D, F#, A and C.

Example 3a:

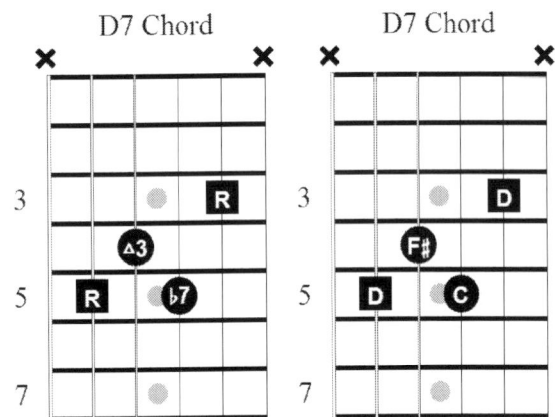

The 'triangle 3' symbol is shorthand for 'major 3rd'.

As you can see, this voicing of D7 doesn't include the 5th of the chord (A).

Here is the extended scale of D Mixolydian (the parent scale of D7).

D	E	F#	G	A	B	C	D	E	F#	G	A	B	C	D
1	2	3	4	5	6	b7	1/8	9	3	11	5	13	b7	1

We can use this voicing of D7 to form a dominant 9 or '9' chord. All we need to do is add the 9th of the scale (E) to the chord. The easiest way to do this is to move the higher-octave root (D) up by one tone and replace it with an E.

Example 3b:

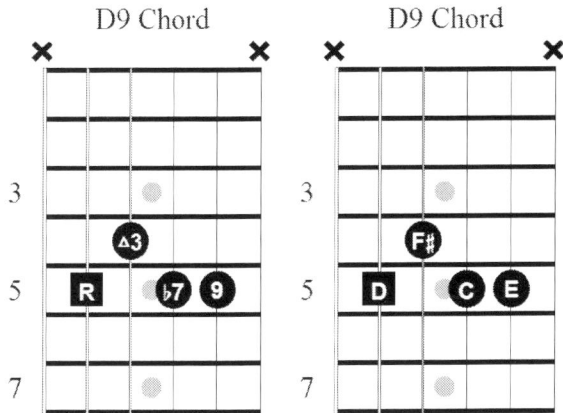

Look carefully to make sure you understand how I replaced the root of the chord with the 9th of the chord to form a dominant 9 or '9' chord.

The intervals contained in this chord voicing are now 1, 3, b7 and 9. We have the 1, 3 and b7 defining the chord as dominant and the 9th (E) creating the *extended* dominant 9th chord.

Dominant 11th or '11' chords are less common and need some special care because the major 3rd of the chord (F#) can easily clash with the 11th (G).

We will gloss over 11th chords for now and come back to them later, although the most common way to form an 11 chord it to lower the 5th of a dominant chord by a tone. The lowering of the 5th is generally voiced one octave above the 3rd otherwise a semitone clash between the 3rd and 11th can occur.

Here is another voicing of a D7 chord, this time it does contain the 5th:

Example 3c:

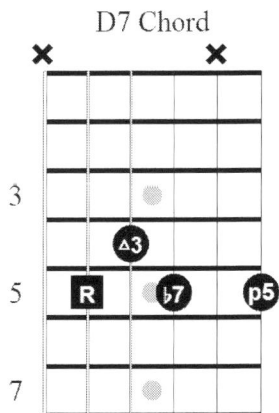

By lowering the 5th (A) by a tone to the 11th (G) we form a dominant 11 or '11' chord.

Example 3d:

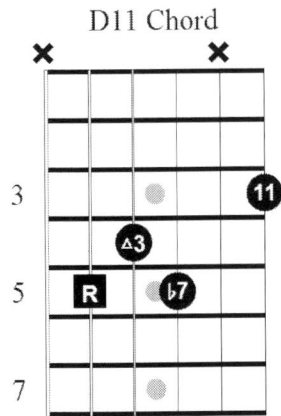

D11 Chord

Dominant 13 chords are much more common in jazz than dominant 11 chords. They are normally created by raising the 5th of a dominant 7 chord by one tone so that it becomes the 13th (6th). It is common to include the 9th of the scale in a 13th chord, but it is by no means necessary.

By combining the last two ideas we can form a D9 chord with the fifth on the 1st string of the guitar:

Example 3e:

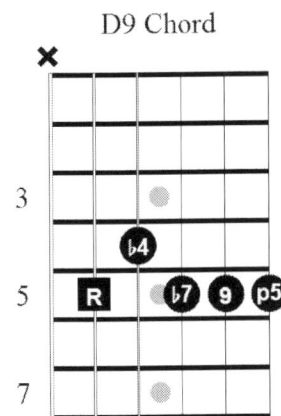

D9 Chord

By raising the 5th by a tone we can reach the 13th degree (interval) of the scale. The chord is given first with the intervals shown, and then with the recommended fingering:

Example 3f:

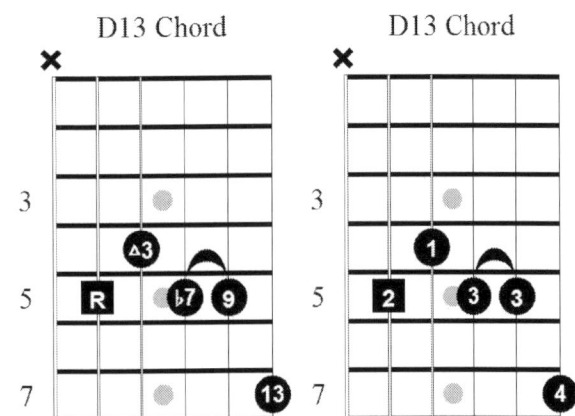

D13 Chord   D13 Chord

As I'm sure you're starting to see, adding extensions to dominant chords is simply a case of knowing where the desired extension is located on the fretboard and then moving a nonessential chord tone to that location.

The above 13 chord can also be voiced slightly differently to achieve a subtly different flavour. We could replace the 9th with the 3rd:

Example 3g:

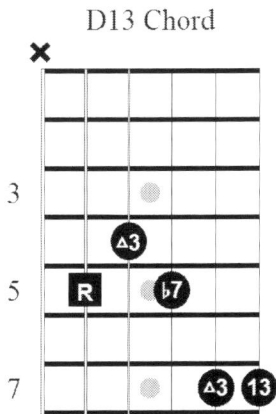

In this voicing there are two 3rd which is completely acceptable. You will probably find the preceding version with the 9th included to be a slightly richer sound.

This approach can also be applied to a dominant 7 chord voiced from the 6th string of the guitar. Here are the root, 3 and b7 of a D7 chord with a 6th string root:

Example 3h:

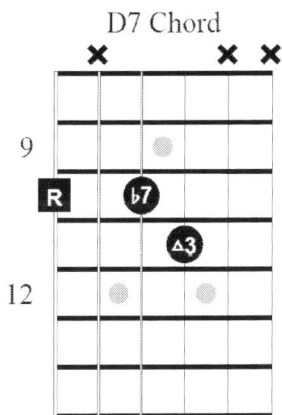

The 5th and higher octave root of this chord are located here:

D7 Chord

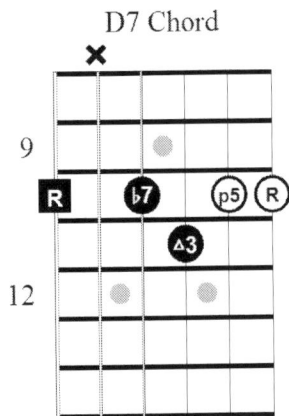

If you remember, we can raise the 5th by a tone to play the 13th of the chord, and we can raise the root of the chord by a tone to target the 9th.

Example 3i:

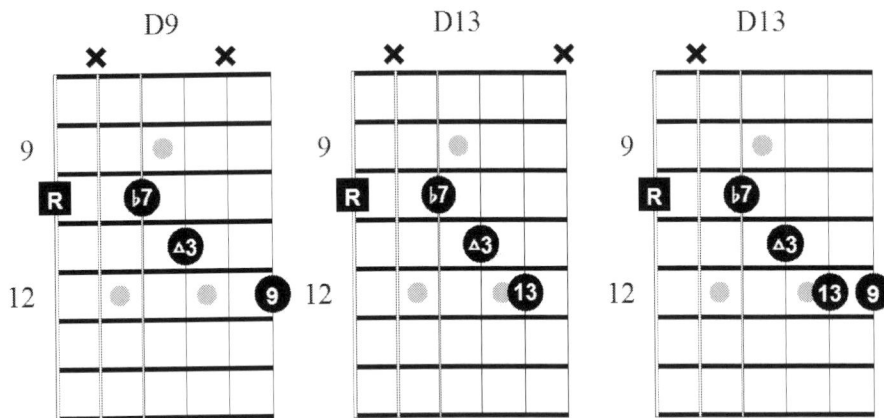

The third diagram shows a 13 chord which includes the 9th. It is still a 13th chord whether or not the 9th is present.

The following two 'shell' voicings are extremely useful fingerings to know, as it is easy to add extensions to them while keeping the root of the chord in the bass. However, as you will learn in chapter fourteen, diatonic extensions are often added by the clever use of chord *substitutions* that replace the original chord.

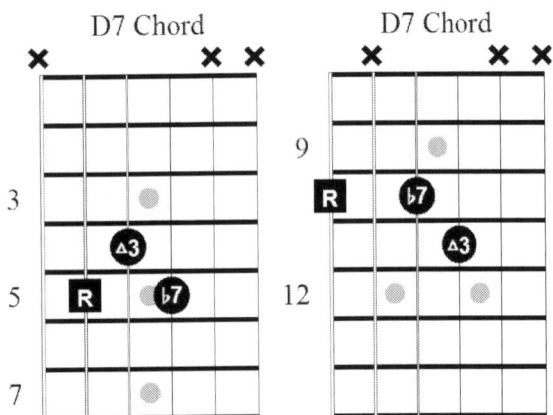

Chapter Four: Chromatic Alterations to Dominant Chords

While diatonic extensions (9, 11 and 13) are added to a dominant chord, it is also extremely common to add *altered* or *chromatic* extensions to a dominant chord. These alterations occur mainly at points of tension in a jazz progression, such as the dominant chord in a ii V I (two, five, one) sequence.

A chromatic alteration is a note that is added to a dominant chord that is not a 9, 11 or 13. We can account for *every* possible chromatic alteration by simply raising or flattening the 9th or 5th of the chord, in fact there are only really four possible altered extensions; b5, #5, b9 and #9.

To see why this is true, let's look at a little bit of theory. Here is the two octave scale of C Mixolydian, the parent scale of C7:

C	D	E	F	G	A	Bb	C	D	E	F	G	A	Bb	C
1	2	3	4	5	6	b7	1/8	9	3	11	5	13	b7	1

And here it is laid out on the guitar neck:

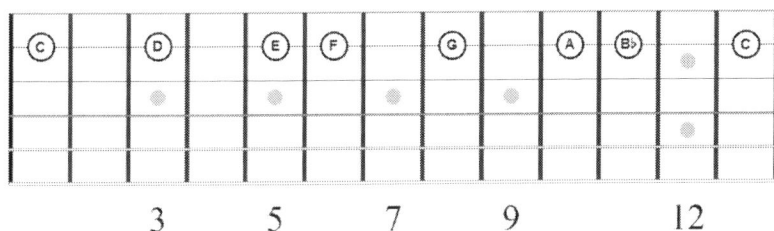

The 5th of the scale is the note G and the 9th is the note D.

I can sharpen the 5th (G) to become a G# to create a #5 tension. I could also achieve the same result by flattening the 6th or 13th note (A) to become an Ab/G#.

For this reason, a b13 interval is exactly the same as a #5. The chords C7#5 and C7b13 are the same.

If you look at the fretboard again, you will see that a #11 (F#) is identical to a b5 (Gb).

A similar thing happens with the 9th of the scale however in any dominant chord you would *never* flatten the 3rd because it would change the quality of the chord from dominant to minor 7.

Remember dominant = 1 3 5 b7, and minor 7 = 1 b3 5 b7. By flattening the 3rd of a dominant chord we have changed the chord quality and it is no longer dominant, unless there is another major 3rd sounding in the chord.

I can sharpen the 9th (D) to become a D# and create a C7#9 sound. I can also flatten the 9th to Db to create a 7b9 sound.

Unlike the 3rd however, it is acceptable to remove the root note from any chord, so as you will see in chapter 9, it is possible to raise the root by a semitone to create a b9 sound.

We cannot raise the b7 of the chord because it would change the chord quality from dominant 7 to major 7.

In summary: b5 = #11 and #5 = b13 so the only true altered extensions to a dominant chord are b5, #5, b9 and #9. You will see chords written down like C7#11b13. This isn't wrong, it's just a question of terminology. The key is to realise that C7#9b13 is the same as C7#9#5.

The reason I teach b5, #5, b9, #9 is because it makes the chords much easier to understand and play on the fretboard.

Working with a D7 chord, to make these examples easier to play, here is a fretboard diagram showing the 1 3 b7 shell voicing of a dominant chord in black, and the 5th and 9th intervals marked in white:

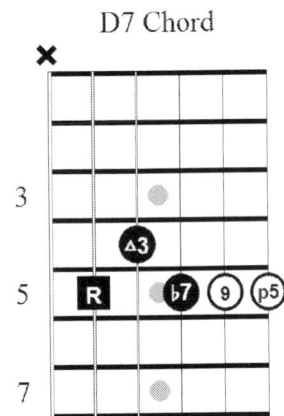

D7 Chord

I can create *any* altered extension by simply moving the white notes up or down by one semitone.

Example 4a:

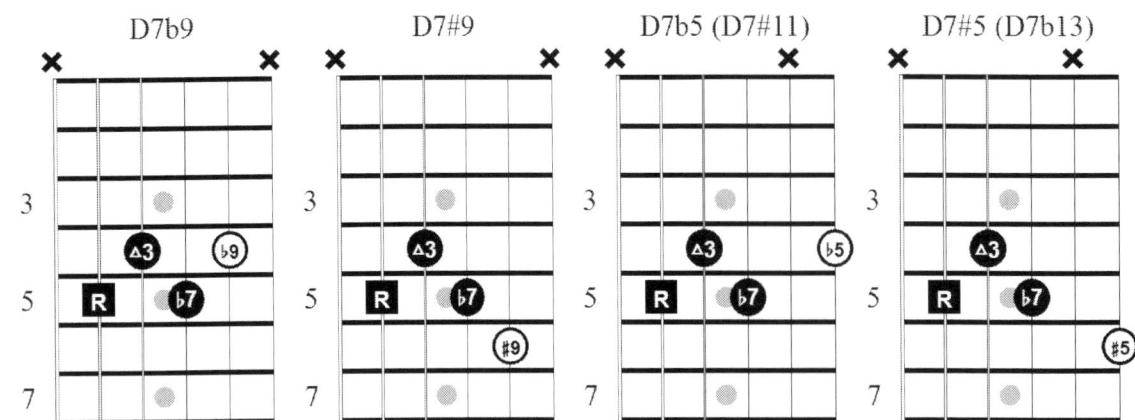

D7b9   D7#9   D7b5 (D7#11)   D7#5 (D7b13)

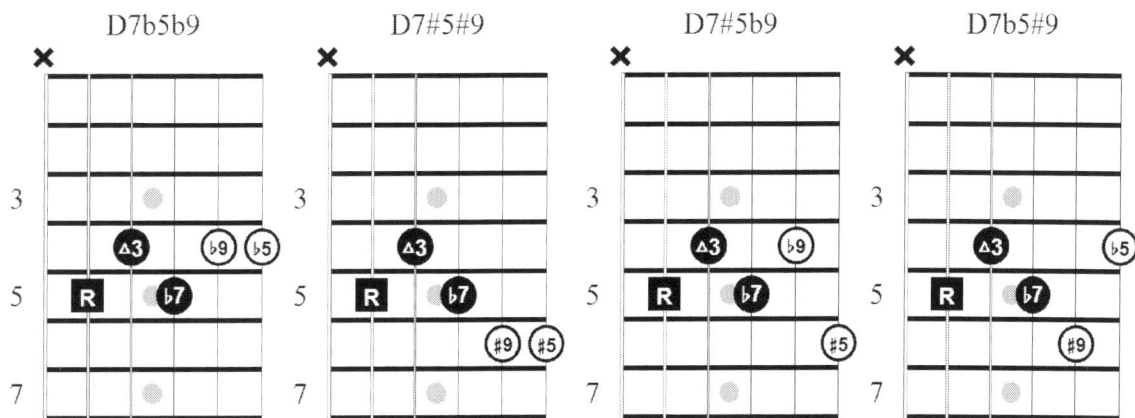

The same is true when we use the dominant 7 shell voicing with a root on the 6th string:

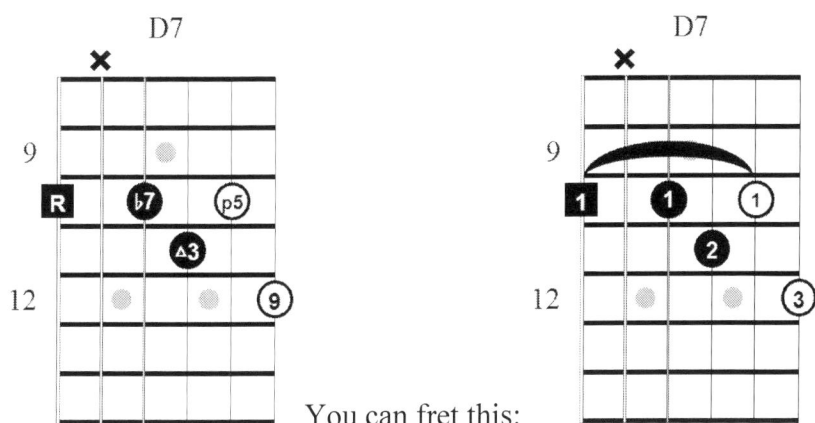

You can fret this:

Some of the altered extensions in this position can be a little hard to reach so quite often these voicings are played rootless. Here are a few of the altered extension permutations available in this position.

Example 4b:

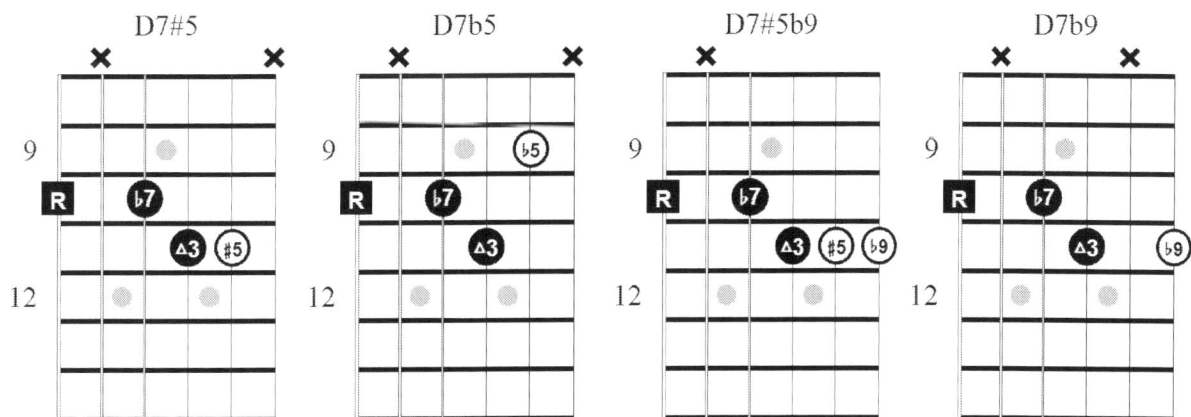

D7#5#9 (rootless)   **D13#9 (rootless)**

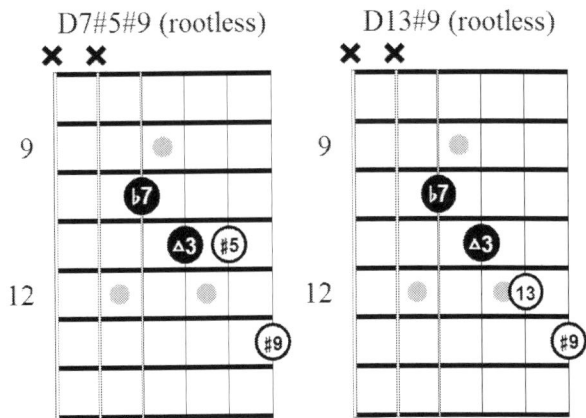

These approaches can be taken with a dominant 7 chord with the root on the 4th string too, although in the basic root position voicing we learnt earlier, we must omit the root when adding a #9 or b9.

The following example uses a G7 chord as the basis for the alterations.

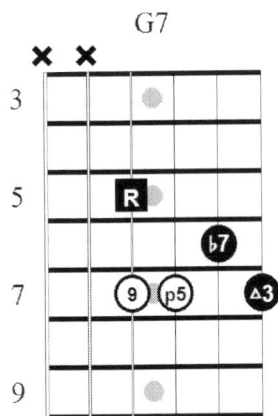

G7

The easiest alterations to add are the #5 and b5, although often the root note will be raised a semitone to create a rootless 7b9 chord.

Example 4c:

G7#5   **G7b5**   **G7b9 (rootless)**   **G7b5b9 (rootless)**

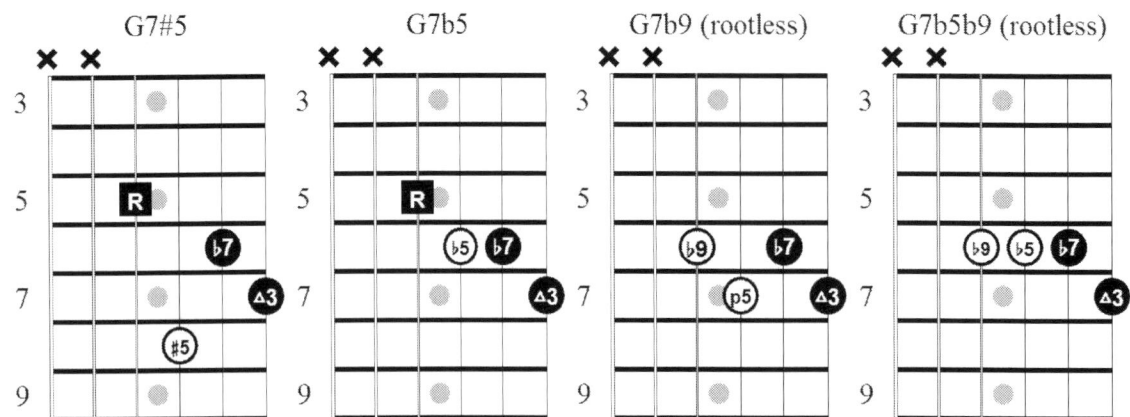

Quite often in jazz chord charts you will simply see the symbol 'alt'. For example 'D7alt'. This means that the composer has not specified a particular altered extension for a dominant 7 chord and so you can use whichever one you feel works best with the music.

It is also important to know that just because a chord chart says '7' it doesn't mean that the chord must be played as a 'straight' 7 chord. If the dominant chord is *static* (not moving), it is normally fine to add in as many natural extensions as you like. For example, four bars of D7 could be played like this:

Example 4d:

D13	D9	D13	D7

If a dominant 7 chord is *functional* (resolving to another chord) then a basic '7' chord can normally be substituted for any dominant chord with a natural extension *or* chromatic alteration.

A chord progression like this:

Example 4e:

Am7	D7	GMaj7	E7

Could be played in any or more of the following ways:

Example 4f:

Am7	D7b9	GMaj7	E7#5b9

Example 4g:

Am7	D7b5b9	GMaj7	E7#5#9

Example 4h:

Am7	D9	GMaj7	E7b5#9

Try playing through the following examples beginning from different root notes, and substitute any diatonic or chromatic extensions you like for the dominant chords you have learnt already.

1)

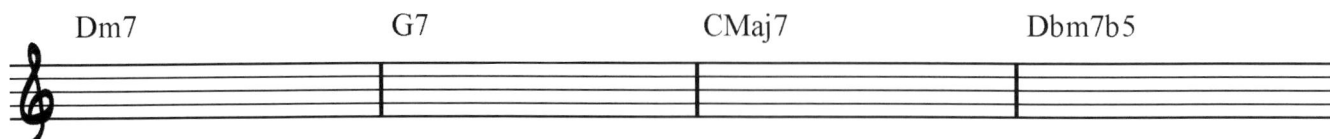

2)

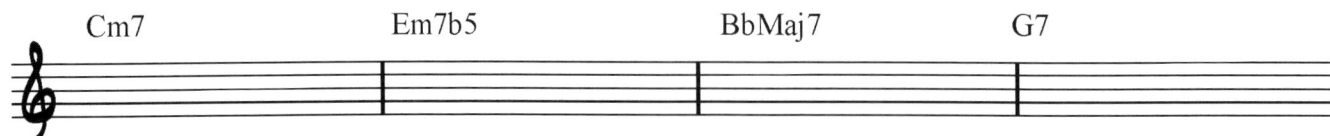

3)

We can take the same approach when adding chromatic alterations to major 7, minor 7 and m7b5 chords, the secret is simply to know where the alterations are on the fretboard.

In the next chapter we will look in more detail at shell or 'guide tone' voicings of the four basic chord types and look at how we can use simple shapes to deal with complex extensions.

Chapter Five: Root and Guide Tone Voicings

As we have already learnt, guide tones are the 3rd and 7th of any chord. Even without playing the root, we can almost completely define a chord by just its 3rd and 7th. You will learn in book two that two related dominant chords can share the same set of guide tones, but for now we can define almost any chord by its root, 3rd and 7th.

To recap,

Chord Type	Interval Formula
Major 7	1 3 5 7
Dominant 7	1 3 5 b7
Minor 7	1 b3 5 b7
Minor 7b5	1 b3 b5 b7

A slight complication arises with the minor 7b5 chord because it has the same guide tones as a minor 7 chord. This is not necessarily a problem because although they *share* the same guide tones, by playing just the b3 and b7 we are not defining whether the 5th is natural or flattened. In other words, we are not adding any extra information and the guide tones sound fine whether the chord is m7 or m7b5.

We could also just add the b5 into the m7b5 voicing as you will see in this chapter.

We will begin by examining a fretboard diagram with a root note marked, and the b3, 3, b7 and 7 highlighted.

This example is in the key of C.

Guide Tones from
a 6th String Root

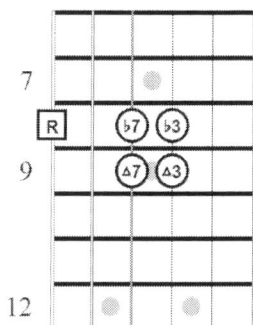

By playing the root note and any 3rd or 7th we can define the most important tones in any chord.

Example 5a:

Maj7 Guide Tones Root 6th String   '7' Guide Tones Root 6th String   m7 Guide Tones Root 6th String   m7b5 Guide Tones Root 6th String

Play through the above examples and listen to the effect that changing only one note has on each voicing. Can you hear the qualities of each chord described by just these three pitches?

Of course, you will have noticed that the m7 and m7b5 chords share the same guide tones as mentioned in the introduction. Don't worry about this for now, but if you are desperate to hear the guide tone voicing with the added b5, you can play the following chord:

m7b5 Guide Tones Root 6th String

Try playing through the following progression using just these root and guide tone voicings based on the 6th string.

You can hear it in **example 5b:**

Gm7b5   C7   Fm7   Dbmaj7

Now we will move on to look at root and guide tone voicings with a 5th string root.

Here is the fretboard overview:

Guide Tones from a
5th String Root

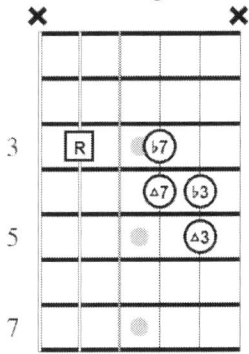

And here are the root and guide tone voicings for each chord.

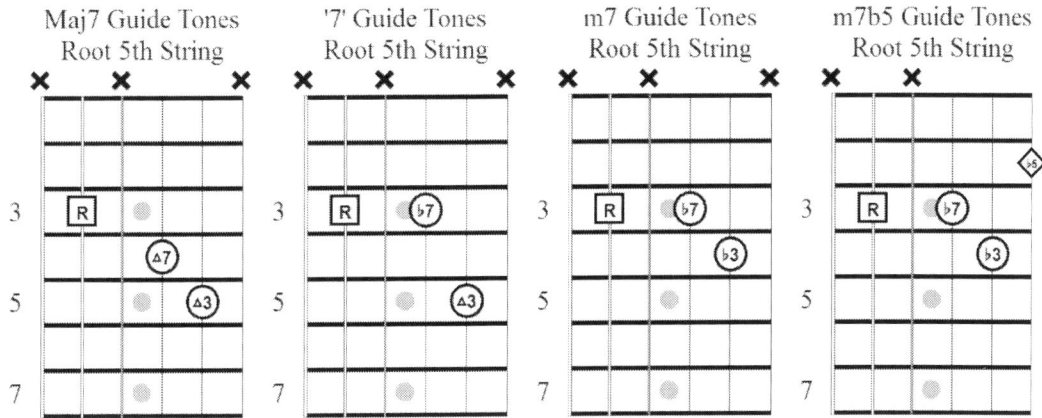

Maj7 Guide Tones
Root 5th String

'7' Guide Tones
Root 5th String

m7 Guide Tones
Root 5th String

m7b5 Guide Tones
Root 5th String

Once again, in the m7b5 diagram, the b5 is **not** a guide tone and is optional. For now I would suggest ignoring it.

Once again, play through the following progression just using root and guide tone voicings on the 5th string:

| Gm7b5 | C7 | Fm7 | Dbmaj7 |

It is important to know that in this position, the 3rds in each chord can be played on the fourth string, one octave lower. By playing the 3rd on the fourth string, we can use the following map of guide tones:

Guide Tones from a 5th String Root

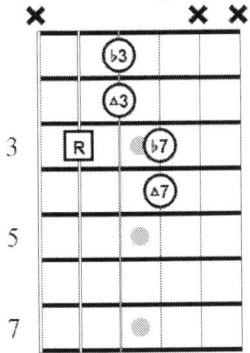

(chord diagram: 5th string root with ♭3, △3, R, ♭7, △7 markings, frets 3, 5, 7)

This means that the previous root and guide tone chords can be played:

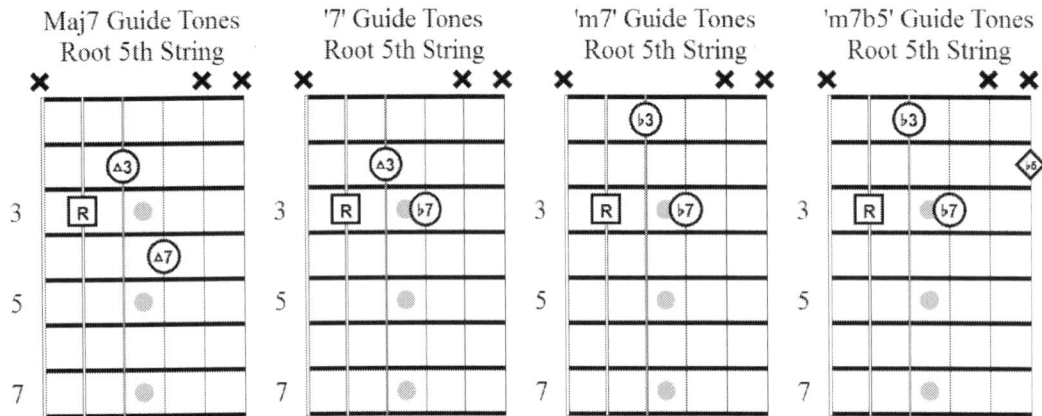

Maj7 Guide Tones Root 5th String — *(diagram with △3, R, △7)*

'7' Guide Tones Root 5th String — *(diagram with △3, R, ♭7)*

'm7' Guide Tones Root 5th String — *(diagram with ♭3, R, ♭7)*

'm7b5' Guide Tones Root 5th String — *(diagram with ♭3, R, ♭7, ♭5)*

Now, let's combine the root and guide tone voicings from both the 6th and 5th string roots and play through the same sequence in a much smoother movement:

Example 5c:

(notation and tablature)

Gm7b5   C7   Fm7   Dbmaj7

```
Gm7b5      C7       Fm7      Dbmaj7
--11------|--------|--9-----|--------|
--10------|--9-----|--8-----|--10----|
--10------|--8-----|--8-----|--10----|
          |--8-----|        |--9-----|
```

Try this approach starting on the 6th string also:

Example 5d:

Or

Example 5e:

Listen to the difference between using different voicings of the root and guide tones. The voicings with the 3rd on the second string tend to be a little brighter than the ones with the 3rd on the fourth string.

Finally, we can learn the guide tone voicings with a root on the fourth string:

As you can see, once again there are two options as to where we voice the 3rd, either on the third string or on the first string. They're both good voicings but playing the 3rd on the first string creates slightly easier fingerings. Experiment to find your favourite sounds and voicings.

The four chord types can be voiced with a fourth string root in the following ways:

Maj 7 Guide Tones
Root 4th String

'7' Guide Tones
Root 4th String

m7 Guide Tones
Root 4th String

m7b5 Guide Tones
Root 4th String

Again, begin by playing through the same chord just using the voicings with the root on the 4th string:

Gm7b5   C7   Fm7   Dbmaj7

Then try combining 4th string and 5th string roots. Here is one possible route through the changes:

Example 5f:

Gm7b5   C7   Fm7   Dbmaj7

Finally, try combining all three string groups and find as many routes through the changes as you can. Here is one beginning from the 4th string.

Example 5g:

Gm7b5   C7   Fm7   Dbmaj7

Try taking the same approach with the following progressions:

1)

| Dm7 | | Em7b5 | A7 | Dm7 | | Bb7 | A7 | DMaj7 |

2)

| Dm7 | | G7 | | CMaj7 | | Dbm7b5 |

3)

| Cm7 | | Em7b5 | | BbMaj7 | | G7 |

Root and guide tone voicings are extremely useful when comping jazz guitar rhythm, especially when you're playing with a bigger band or any line up where there is a piano. Pianos and horn sections can often provide a great deal of harmonic information, and by overplaying on the guitar we can sometimes clash with these other instruments unless parts are worked out quite carefully.

By playing root and guide tone voicings we are playing just the basic (yet important) chord information and we can focus more on providing a musical rhythmic accompaniment to the ensemble.

In the next chapter we will look at how we can remove even the root notes from these voicings before learning to add in natural extensions and chromatic alterations to the basic shell voicings.

Chapter Six: Using Rootless Guide Tone Voicings

As mentioned in the previous chapter, the defining notes of any chord are the 3rd and 7th. If we only play these two intervals we can define almost any chord. In this chapter we will look at how we can convey the correct harmonic information, even in very complex progressions, with just two notes on each chord.

Consider the following progression:

Cm7	F7b9	Bm7	E7b9	Bbm7	Eb7#9	AbMaj7

From what we have learnt so far, we have quite a few approaches we can take when playing this line of chords.

One solution could be the following sequence.

Example 6a:

These chord voicings work very well in a small band setting, perhaps when accompanying a singer or in a small trio without a piano.

If the band gets bigger it is often likely that we will want to reduce the amount of notes we are playing and let other instruments take care of extensions and alterations. It is likely that there is another instrument playing a bass line, possibly an upright bass or organ pedals.

In these contexts guitarists often reduce the amount of notes they are playing to just guide tone voicings without the root.

You have already learnt where these notes lie on the guitar neck in conjunction with the chord root, but now let's try playing them in isolation and see if we can still 'hear' the harmony of the chord progression implied by these chord tones.

To play these voicings, *visualise* the roots of each guide tone voicing shape, but don't actually play them. It may help you at first to finger the full chord, but only strum or pick the desired tones.

One way to play through the previous progression using guide tone shapes is shown in the following example. I am visualising the roots of the chords on the 6th and 5th strings:

Example 6b:

When you have this example under your fingers, compare examples 6a and 6b. Play through example 6a and then immediately play through example 6b. While example 6b certainly doesn't have the 'richness' of example 6a, you can certainly hear the harmony moving as described in the chord symbols.

By using guide tones in this way we can easily convey the important information in a chord sequence while leaving a lot of room for other instruments in the band to play their parts.

The previous example throws up an interesting and important point. As you may know, the 'ii V I' (two five one) progression is the most common chord sequence played in jazz music. The ii V I is formed when we harmonise the 2nd, 5th and root degrees of a major scale. It is rare to find a jazz standard that doesn't include at least one, if not many ii V I progressions.

The final two bars of example 6b form a standard ii V I progression. As this chord sequence occurs so often in jazz it is very important to start forming a 'dictionary' of different ways to play these chords. Using rootless guide tone voicings in this way is one of the simplest ways to navigate the chord sequence as we only change one note each time.

In a normal ii V I, the b7 of the ii chord will *always* fall by a semitone to become the 3rd of the V chord. The b3 of the ii chord stays the same and becomes the b7 of the V chord.

When the V chord moves to the I chord, the b7 of the V chord will always fall by a semitone to become the 3rd of the I chord. The 3rd of the V chord stays the same and becomes the 7th of the I chord.

This is easier to see in the following diagram.

b7 falls to 3   b7 falls to 3

Knowing that this movement is always the same in a ii V I is very useful as it allows us to make the smallest possible movement to define a new chord. It is also a great way to start to learn how chord intervals move on the guitar neck as chords change. This is fantastic when it comes to soloing as we already know where the strongest notes from each chord lie on the guitar.

Look back to the first two bars of example 6b. Can you see that these chords are a series of unresolved 'ii Vs'?

The guide tones have the same movement as the chords in bar three, but they do not resolve to a tonic maj7 chord as the final chords.

This kind of sequence is very common in jazz and it is used in tunes such as Blues for Alice by Charlie Parker where there are many substitutions to the original harmony.

Study bars one and two of example 6b to make sure you understand how the guide tones are moving. Notice that in these cycles, only one note is moving each time.

Try playing through example 6b using guide tones based off the 5th and 4th strings. Remember to only visualise the root note, don't play it.

Another common chord progression in jazz is the 'vi ii V I' (six, two, five, one) sequence. The chord *qualities* often vary in this sequence (often VI and ii are played as dominant chords) but in its natural form the vi chord is a minor 7 (hence the small Roman numeral figure: vi denotes minor, VI denotes major, VI7 denotes a 7 chord).

A vi ii V I sequence in the key of G might look like this:

We have looked at a few ways you could play through this sequence, however if we reduce it to just guide tone voicings we could play it like this

Example 6c:

As I mentioned before, the qualities of these chord progressions often change. Here is an example of the same sequence but this time each chord is played as a dominant 7.

Example 6d:

Try playing the above example both with and without the roots, and also play it while visualising the root of the E chord on the 6th string (12th fret). You will notice that you only need to move the guide tones down by a semitone (one fret) each time to play through this entire sequence.

Practice using guide tone voicings without roots on all the examples in previous chapters. You can also easily find jazz chord charts online or in a 'fake' book. In particular, you might want to begin by studying jazz blues tunes such as Billie's Bounce or Blues for Alice, and Rhythm Changes tunes, such as I Got Rhythm or Anthropology as they contain a lot of common chord movements.

Try playing complete tunes just on adjacent string sets, i.e., the 2nd and 3rd and 3rd and 4th strings. Keep your guide tone movements as close and as smooth as possible. Remember to ignore any natural or chromatic extensions to chords. If you see any major 6 or minor 6 chords, for now play them as Major 7 or minor 7 chords.

The more practice you do at this kind of rhythm playing, the deeper your understanding of jazz chord movements will become. Breaking a jazz tune down into its essential elements is an excellent way to *hear* the tune properly, and this will in turn lead to better chord playing and soloing.

One other reason that guitarists like rootless guide tone voicings on the middle strings is that they give us lots of room to add walking basslines below, and melodies above the basic harmony. We will look at these concepts in book three.

Chapter Seven: Rootless Guide Tone Voicings with Extensions

It is common to use voicings that consist of 'rootless guide tones plus an extension'. In this scenario we will play the guide tones as we did in the previous chapter and add a little colour by selecting an appropriate extension or chromatic alteration.

This idea is an extremely easy way to add depth and richness to your comping without overpowering the rest of the band. The secret is to know your fretboard in terms of intervals from any root note.

We will begin by picking a root note and learning where all the natural extensions lie in relation to it. As it is a common jazz key, we will work in the key of Bb.

Natural Extensions
6th String Root

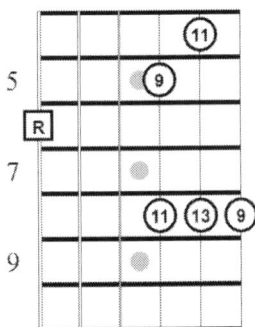

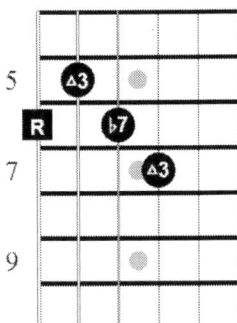

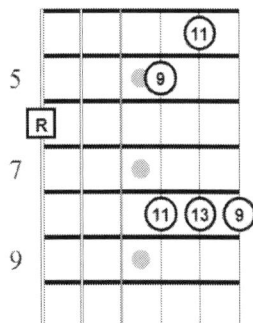

The notes on the 3rd string may not always be very useful to us as often we will be playing a guide tone on that string, although there will be some occasions where we wish to omit the 3rd of a chord in favour of the 11th.

Don't forget we can also move the 3rd of the guide tone voicing to the 5th string if we need to access an extension on the 3rd string although this kind of voicing can be quite bassy and muddy in a low register.

To refresh our memory, here are the guide tones of a Bb7 chord placed next to the extensions in the previous diagram:

'7 'Guide Tones   Natural Extensions
6th String Root   6th String Root

We can now combine these diagrams when we wish to play a guide tone plus extension voicing.

For example, here are two great voicings of a Bb9 chord.

Example 7a:

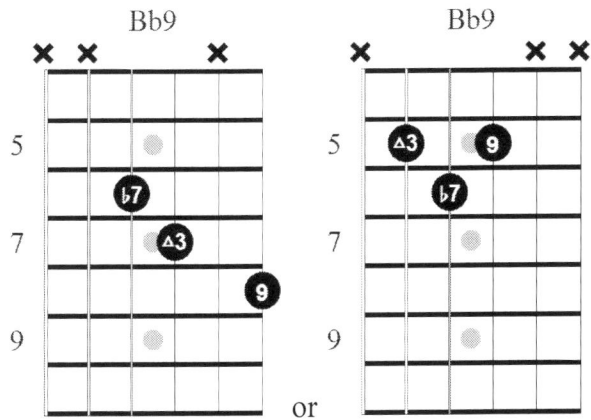

or

The following is an excellent '13' voicing.

Example 7b:

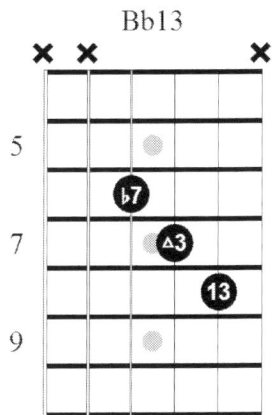

You could play a 'true' Bb11 chord in the following way.

Example 7c:

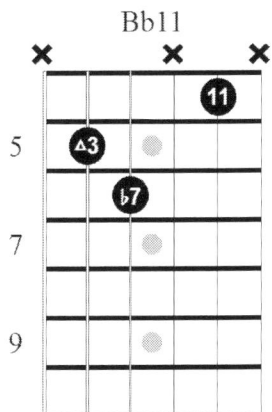

'11' chords often need to be handled with care as the 11th/4th is only a semitone distance away from the major 3rd. Always try to put them in different octaves. Also, it is important to note that 11 chords are similar but not the same as a 7sus4 chord. Both chords include the 11th (4th), however a 7sus4 chord omits the root to form a suspended chord. In this case we can simply raise the 3rd by a semitone to account for the sus4.

The following diagrams clarify this concept.

Example 7d:

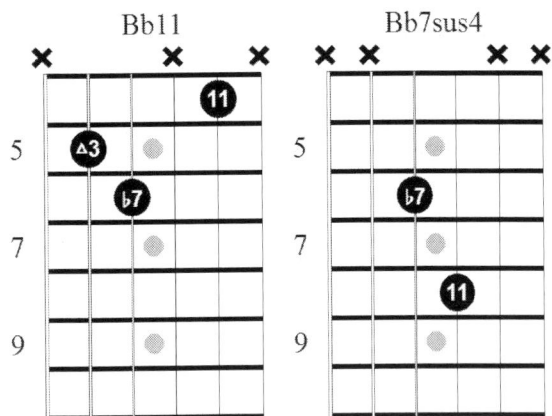

Example 7e:

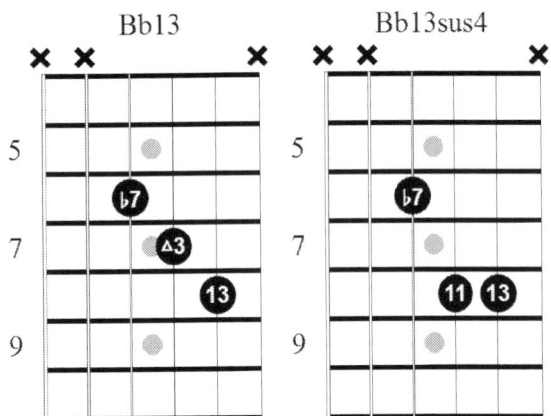

A 'sus' chord does not contain a 3rd. A '9', '11' or '13' chord contains a 3rd plus an extension.

Now let's move on to adding altered extensions to our dominant 7 guide tones.

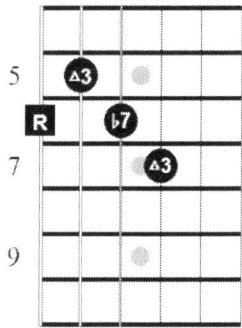

'7 'Guide Tones
6th String Root

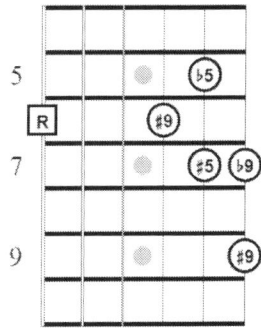

Altered Extensions
6th String Root

Once again, a useful extension (the #9) is located on the 3rd string, so we might have to drop the 3rd down an octave to be able to play this note comfortably. Also, the b9 and #9 that are located on the 1st string can be quite a long way from the guide tone pair. In this case it is sometimes possible to raise the b7 guide tone up by an octave to make a more convenient fingering.

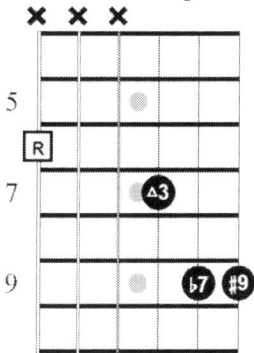

b7 up an octave
#9 voicing

(Don't play the root in this example)

As with all these voicings, the range of the guitar that you use will depend very much on which chord voicings preceded and follow the current one.

Some common altered dominant guide tone plus extension grips are

Example 7f:

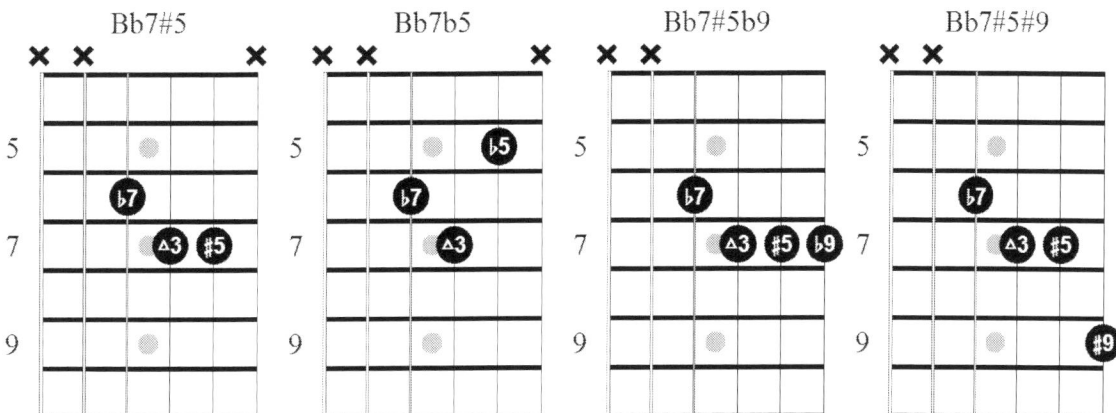

Of course, it is perfectly acceptable to combine natural and altered extensions in this way.

Example 7g:

Bb13b9

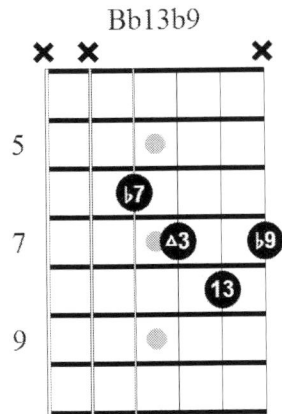

These chord shapes are all movable, so practice playing them in different keys. It is important to visualise them based around the root note on the 6th string.

We will now look at the natural extensions of a dominant 7 chord with a root on the 5th string. Here are the natural and altered extensions of a D7 chord.

Natural Extensions
5th String Root

Altered Extensions
5th String Root

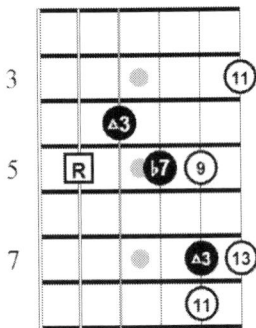

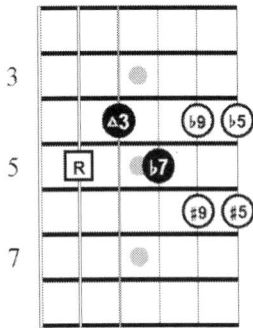

Notice the higher octave 3rd highlighted in the first diagram.

Using these two diagrams, we can construct any natural or altered extension or a combination of the two.

Example 7h:

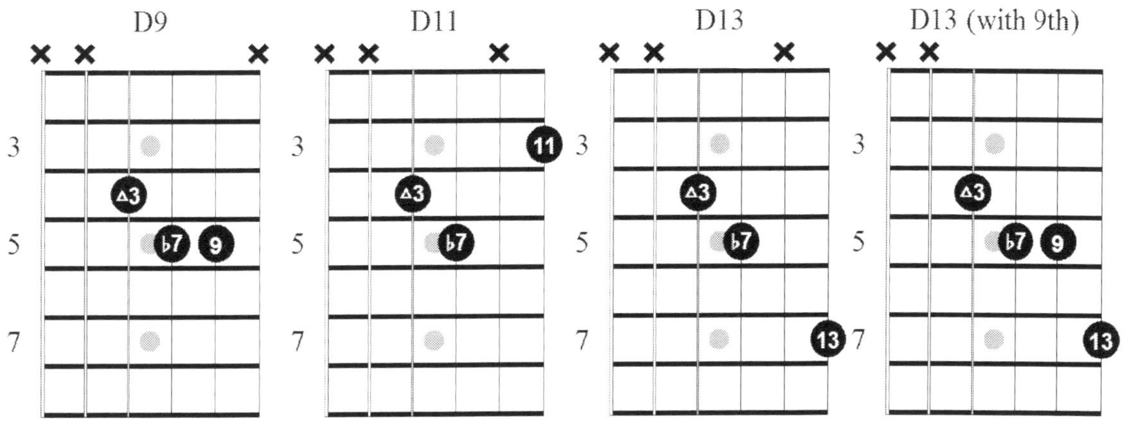

D9   D11   D13   D13 (with 9th)

Example 7i:

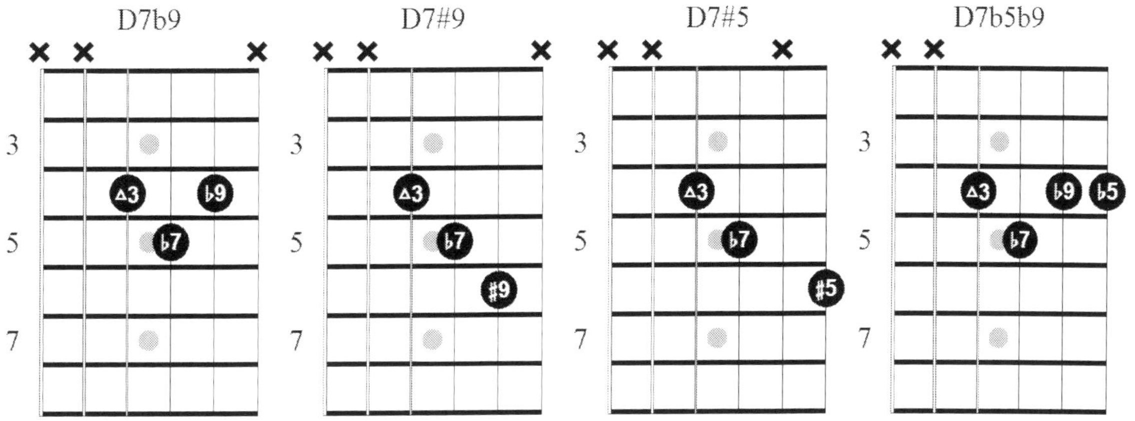

D7b9   D7#9   D7#5   D7b5b9

Example 7j:

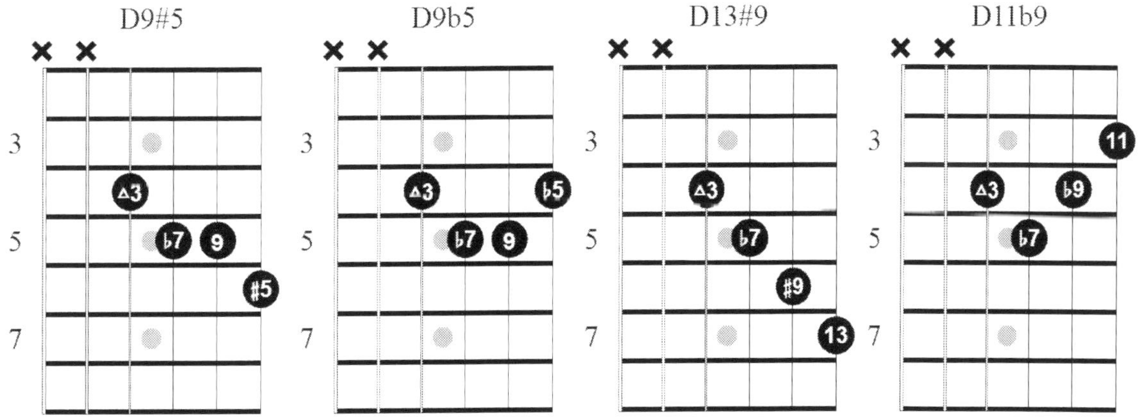

D9#5   D9b5   D13#9   D11b9

Try combining the 6th-string and 5th-string guide-tone-plus-extension voicings over the following chord progressions. See how many ways you can find to navigate the changes.

The following chord sequences can be quite tricky at first. You may wish to add in the root notes to help visualise the chords before later omitting them in order to play just the guide tones and extensions.

Again, find as many jazz chord charts as you can and apply these techniques. You will quickly find yourself starting to see the fretboard purely in terms of intervals from any root note. This is extremely desirable for quick chord construction and articulate soloing.

1)

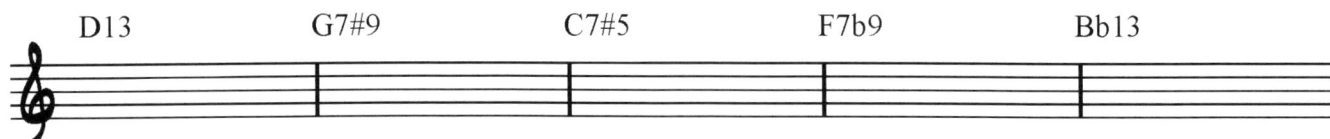

2)

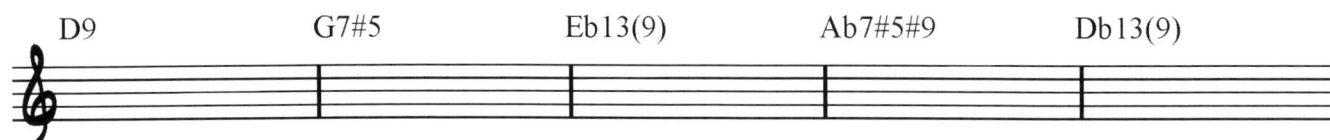

(9) = include the 9th in the 13 chord.

3)

The same extensions apply whether you are using major 7, minor 7 or minor 7b5 guide tones. The following diagrams show all these possibilities with roots on the 6th and 5th strings. They are all shown in the key of C. Root notes are shown by white squares, guide tones are shown by black circles and extensions are shown by white circles.

Minor 7 / Minor 7b5 Guide Tones with Extensions

m7 (b5) Guide Tones
Root 6

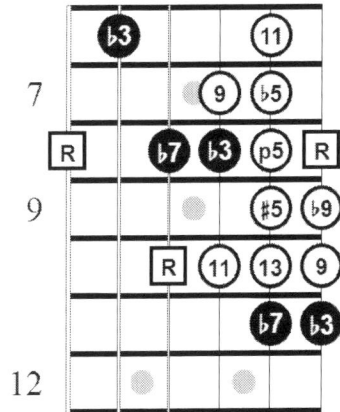

m7 (b5) Guide Tones
Root 5

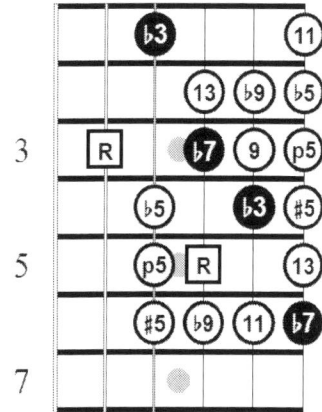

Major 7 Guide Tones with Extensions

Maj7 Guide Tones
Root 6

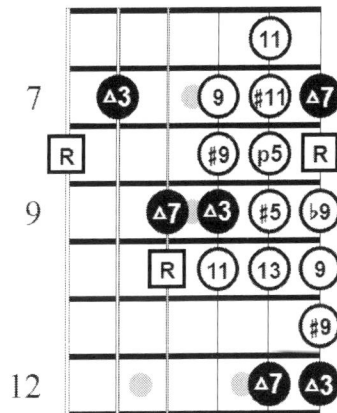

Maj7 Guide Tones
Root 5

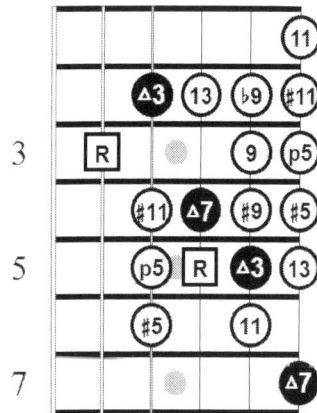

*Maj7#9 and Maj7b9 are both extremely rare to see, although the sixth mode of the harmonic minor scale harmonises to become a maj13#9#11 chord so maj7#9 chords may occasionally crop up. Just make sure that the #9 is voiced an octave above the major 3rd.

With Maj7-type chords, some care must be taken when naming b5 and #11 intervals which are often used interchangeably, although this is theoretically incorrect. Maj7b5 implies that the natural 5th has been replaced with the b5, whereas maj7#11 implies that there could be a natural 5th and a #11 in the chord, although this is not common practice with guitar voicings.

Dominant 7 Guide Tones with Extensions

Dom 7 Guide Tones
Root 6

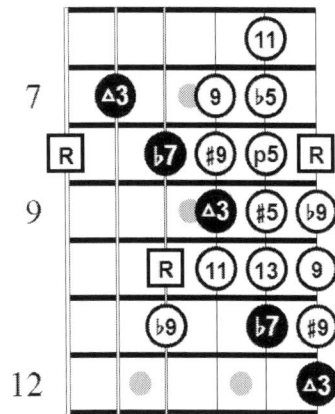

Dom 7 Guide Tones
Root 5

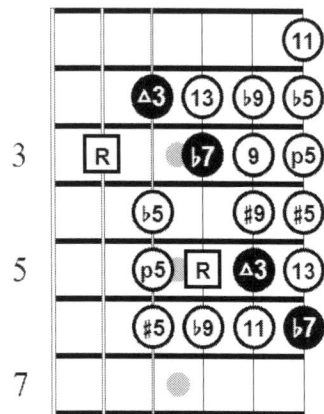

b5 = #11
#5 = b13

These two pages are two of the most useful in this book. They summarise every basic chord voicing and show how any simple or complex chord can be fretted with just three or four notes. I suggest that you copy out the diagrams on these pages and stick them onto the wall where you practice. Make an effort to memorise these intervals and use them in your playing.

Chapter Eight: Applying Extended Guide Tone Voicings

The last three chapters contained a great deal of information that should take a few weeks to memorise and incorporate. It will be useful to look at a few approaches to help you internalise and quickly access these chords.

We will begin by looking at a common chord progression that contains all of the basic four chord types.

Gm7b5   C7   Fm7   Dbmaj7

Begin by making sure you can play this progression with the chord shapes in chapter two with roots on the 6th, 5th and 4th strings, and that you can easily move between chords on adjacent strings. This process is described in detail in chapter two.

Next, play through the chord sequence using just root and guide tone voicings. Find as many possible routes as you can through the changes. This process is described in chapter five.

When you have gained confidence with these voicings move on to adding *just* one extension to each chord. Use the same extension on each chord where possible.

We will begin with '9th' chords and playing the root of the first chord on the 5th string.

Example 8a:

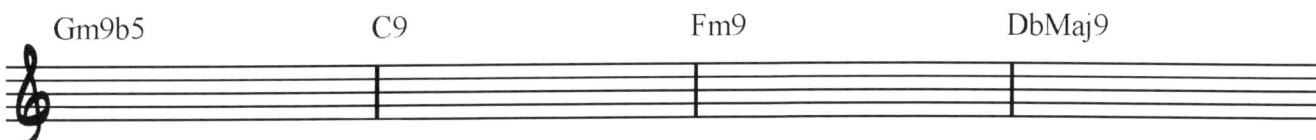

Gm9b5   C9   Fm9   DbMaj9

These chords could be voiced in the following way:

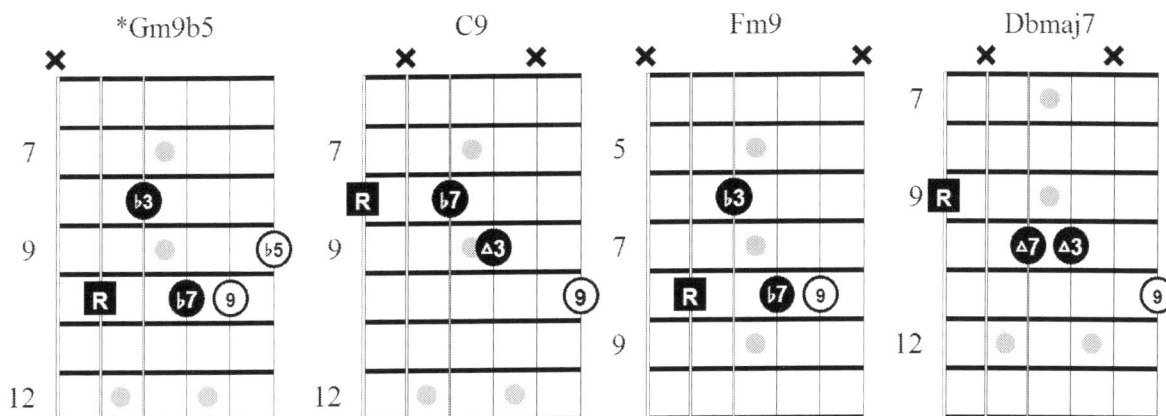

* When practicing guide tone voicings in this way, m7b5 chords always pose a problem. The above Gm9b5 chord is almost impossible to fret so it requires us to leave out one note. If we're sticking to 'true' root + guide tone voicings then we should clearly leave out the b5, but that gives us exactly the same shape as a m9 chord which doesn't really help us to distinguish between the two chords.

We *could* play the b5 on the 5th string as in the following diagram, but that means leaving out the b3. (If we play the b3 on the 2nd string then we can't add the 9th!) This is actually a fairly good choice of voicing; even though the 3rd is not played, the ear seems to fill in the gap.

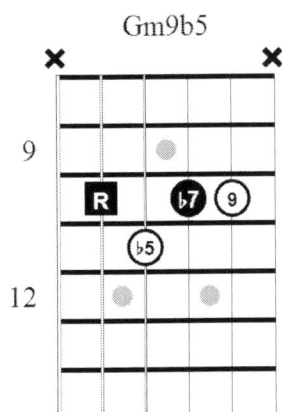

Gm9b5

Another alternative is to omit the root, although that doesn't really fit in to the root and guide tone system we're learning. It is a great voicing in certain contexts, but played in isolation it can easily sound like a min/Maj7 chord with a root on the 4th string:

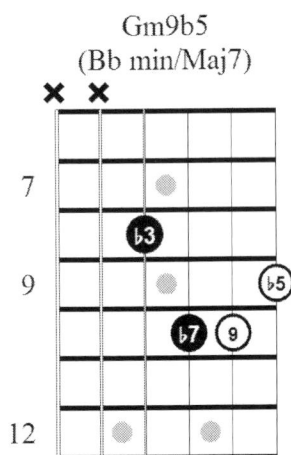

Gm9b5
(Bb min/Maj7)

What's the answer? Well, the truth is there is no consistent way to organise every single chord type due to the organisation of the notes on the guitar neck. My advice would differ depending on your ability and comfort level with this kind of material.

I would definitely suggest that your starting point should be omitting the b5 and fretting the chord with the same shape as the m9 voicing above in order to develop a consistent system. Do, however *visualise* the possible b5 locations and try to incorporate them into your playing at a later stage.

Next, move on to playing each chord as an 11 voicing where possible.

Example 8b:

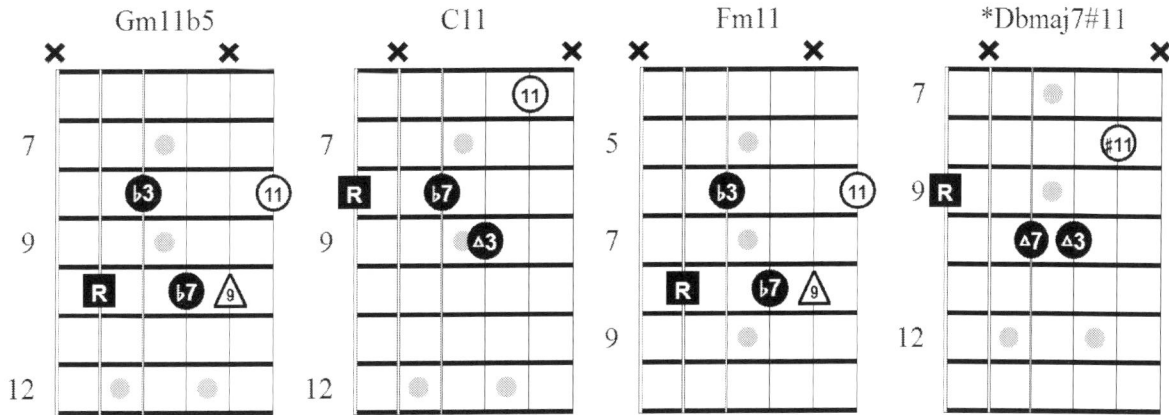

Gm11b5   C11   Fm11   *Dbmaj7#11

Major 7 chords with an added natural 11 are quite rare due to the semitone clash between the 3rd and 11. Most often you will see the 3rd omitted to form a sus4 chord.

Major 7#11 chords are quite common so my suggestion is to begin by using #11s on major 7 chords.

You will notice in some of the diagrams above I have also included the 9ths of the chords in triangles. These are optional and can be added if you wish. Remember that just because a chord says '13' it doesn't mean you can't add in the 9th or 11th. For now though, I suggest you focus on adding just one extension to the guide tones. The idea of this exercise is to allow you to learn the fretboard in terms of intervals. Keeping it simple will speed up the process.

Now repeat the process with '13' chords.

Maj13th chords need attention in their voicing. There is a potential semitone clash between the 13th (6th) and b7th. Make sure the 13th is always in a higher octave than the b7th.

Example 8c:

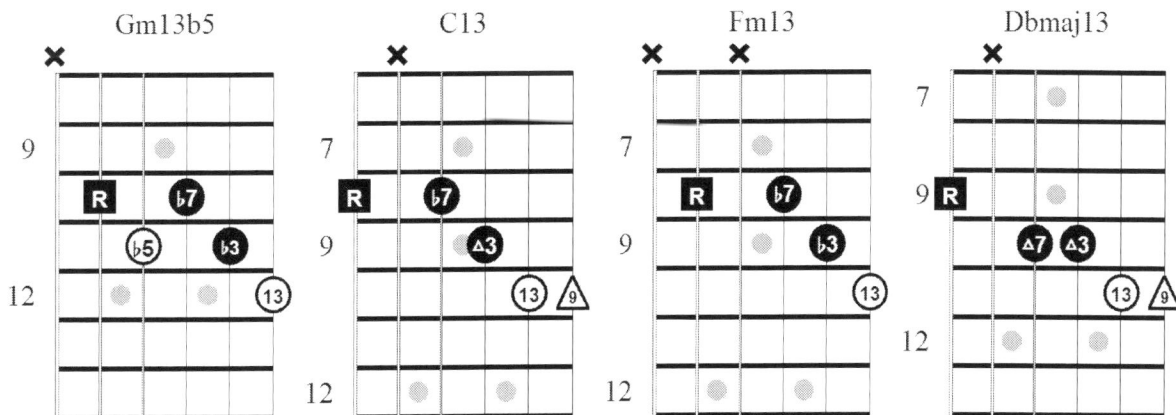

Gm13b5   C13   Fm13   Dbmaj13

Before moving on, repeat this section but this time play through the chord progression using rootless chords.

For example, the previous exercise would be played:

Example 8d:

Gm13b5   C13   Fm13   Dbmaj13

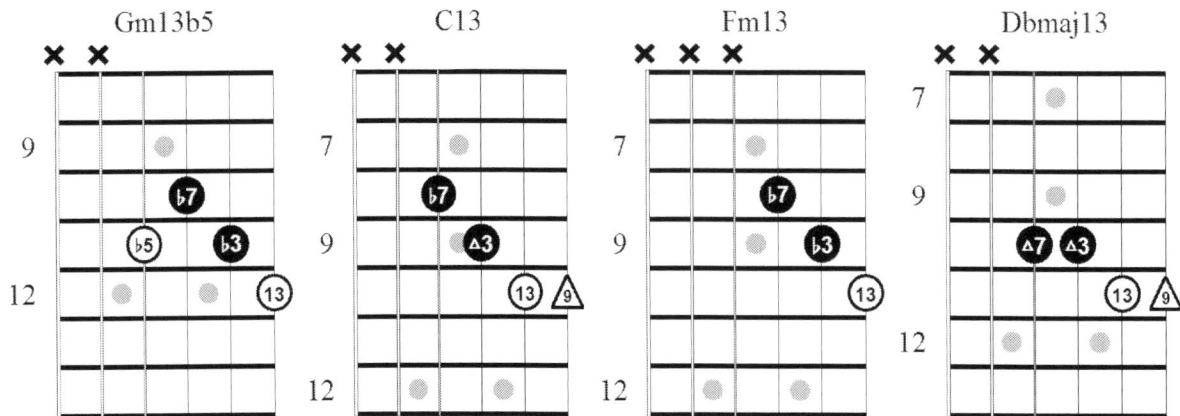

This may seem like overkill, but going through this process will really open up some new fingering possibilities for you and give you many options when you start to add melodies and walking bass ideas in book three. It will also greatly help you to internalise the locations of the intervals on the neck, and later to start recognising common *chord substitutions* which will be tackled in great detail in book two.

Now go through the same steps but apply the process to the chords using voicings starting on the 6th string. This is your starting point for exploration:

Example 8e:

Gm9b5   C9   Fm9   Dbmaj9

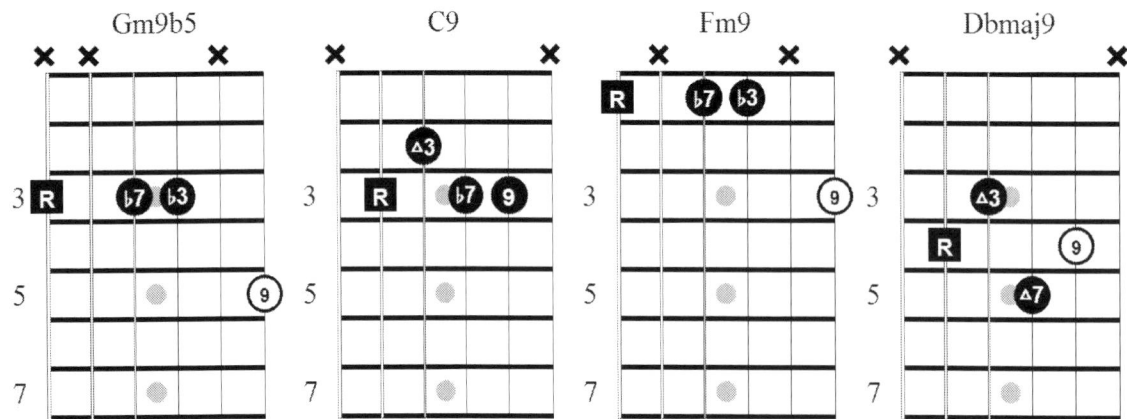

Remember, keep it simple and methodical; the objective is to learn the locations of the extensions in this position.

The next stage is to begin to incorporate altered extensions on to the dominant chords. You can use the previous progression and add altered extensions to the C7 chord, although because there is only one dominant chord in the progression it will take a while to internalise the sounds and permutations available.

I suggest using the following progression to help you introduce altered extensions to the dominant chords.

D7   G7   C7   F7   BbMaj7

Begin by adding one extension for each chord. In the following example I add a #5 (b13) to each dominant chord.

Example 8f:

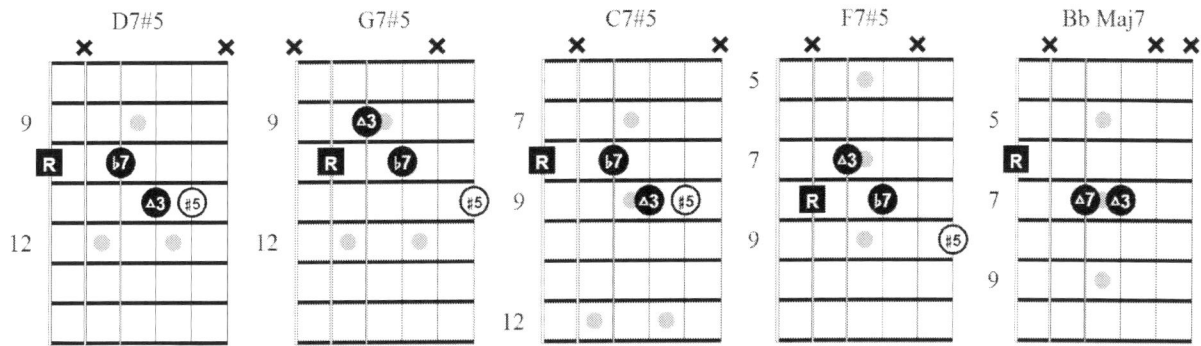

Change the altered extension you add each time and work in both positions on the neck. If you have problems fretting any of the voicings you may have to revert to using rootless voicings occasionally.

As you gain confidence try combining two different altered extensions. The possible combinations are

b5	b9
b5	#9
b5	9
5	b9
5	#9

You can also combine the 13th with an altered extension if the fingering pattern allows it.

Remember that altered extensions are most appropriate for progressions where the dominant chord is *functional*. This means that the dominant chord is moving to another chord, normally one that is the distance of a 4th or 5th away.

When the dominant chord is static it is often inappropriate to add altered extensions in this way, although there are some exceptions to both rules.

The following sets of chord changes are great workhorses for trying out new extension ideas and for developing a range of chord change licks that you can apply to many common jazz progressions.

Line 1: | BbMaj7 | G7 | Cm7 | F7 | Dm7 | G7 | C7 | F7 |

Line 2: | Fm7 | Bb7 | EbMaj7 | Ebm7 | Dm7 | G7 | Cm7 | F7 |

Line 3: | Em7b5 | A7 | Dm7 | | Am7b5 | D7 | Gm7 | |

Line 4: | Bb7 | A7 | Dmaj7 | | | | | |

Of course, there are many, many jazz progressions you can apply these concepts to. Get yourself a copy of The Real Book and pick a few tunes at random to test yourself. This is the best kind of practice.

Chapter Nine: Diminished 7 Chords

Now we have looked at how the most common four '7th' chords are formed and played we will take a look at some structures that fall slightly outside the system we have been using so far. The chords in the following chapters are all very common occurrences in jazz.

We will begin with the diminished 7 chord.

As you learnt in chapter one, a diminished triad consists of the scale intervals 1 b3 b5. A diminished 7 chord adds a bb7 (double flat 7) interval to this triad to give the formula

1 b3 b5 bb7.

In the key of C this formula generates the notes C Eb Gb Bbb (A).

The diminished 7 chord occurs naturally when you harmonise the 7th degree of the harmonic minor scale.

While the bb7 is enharmonically the same note as the 6th, this structure is always seen as a 7th voicing.

When laid out on the fretboard, you will notice that the notes of a diminished chord have an unusual quality.

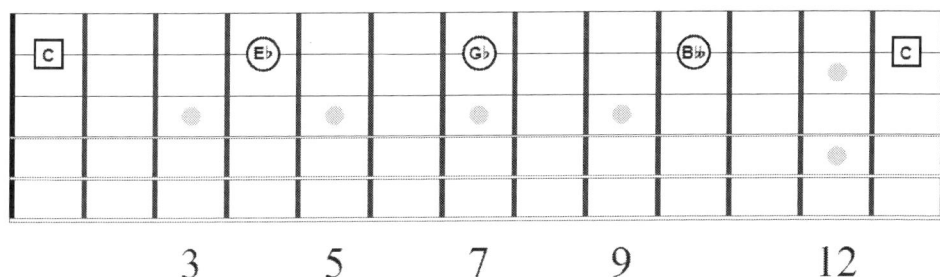

Each note is a minor 3rd (one-and-a-half tones) apart. This has some far-reaching theoretical consequences but for now it is important to realise just one thing:

The notes in the chords of C Dim7, Eb Dim7, Gb Dim7 and A Dim 7 are the same. This symmetry leads to some interesting possibilities in terms of modulation (key changes) which we will study in part three.

Diminished chords have an instantly recognisable sound, and were commonly used in old-fashioned horror movies and by J.S. Bach!

You can fret diminished 7 chords with roots on the 6th, 5th and 4th strings.

Example 9a:

G Diminished 7
Root 6

G Diminished 7
Root 5

G Diminished 7
Root 4

To create that classic Hammer-Horror sound, try moving a diminished 7 chord up or down by the interval of a minor 3rd:

Example 9b:

Try this with each of the three chord voicings above.

While the diminished chord is used as a defined sound in its own right, it is very commonly used as a *substitution* for other chords. We will be taking a detailed look at common chord substitutions in Part Two but we will cover one very important diminished 7 substitution now.

Compare the chords of C7 and C# diminished 7:

Example 9c:

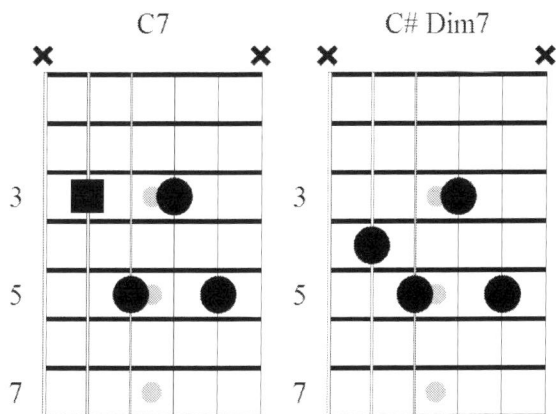

Can you see that the chord of C# diminished contains exactly the same notes as C7, apart from the root, which has been raised by a semitone to become a b9 interval?

You can see this in the following diagram of intervals.

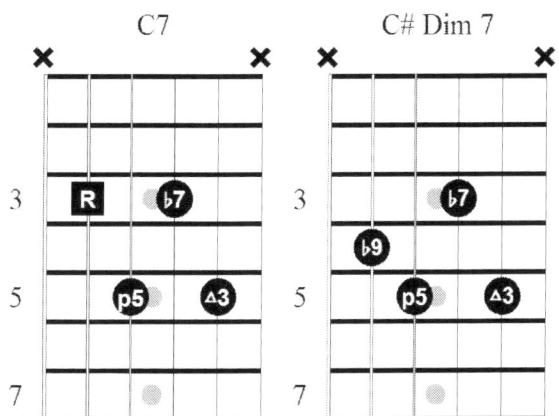

A C# diminished chord contains exactly the same notes as a rootless C7b9 chord. This has been one of the most common substitutions in music for a long time.

For reasons of convenience and for building a consistent system of substitutions, many jazz musicians see this substitution as building a diminished 7 chord on the *3rd* of a dominant chord. Remember, diminished 7 chords are symmetrical so C# diminished 7 contains the same notes as the following chords:

C# Dim7 – E Dim7 – G Dim7 – Bb Dim7.

For reasons that will become clear in chapter fourteen it is normally easier to see a chord substitution built on a chord tone like the 3rd, as opposed to a non-chord tone like the b9, even though they are technically the same thing.

This substitution works beautifully every time you encounter a functional dominant chord. All you need to do to imply a 7b9 chord is play a dim7 chord on the 3rd of the original dominant chord.

For example, in the chord progression

Gm7   C7   FMaj7

We can substitute the chord E dim7 for the C7 chord to create a C7b9 sound:

Example 9d:

Gm7   C# Dim 7   Fm7

Gm7   C7b9 / E Dim7   FMaj7

Because of its symmetrical nature, there is no reason we can't use more than one diminished substitution on the C7 chord. Try moving the diminished chord up by three frets before resolving to the FMaj7 chord:

Example 9e:

Gm7   C7b9 / E Dim7   C7b9 / E Dim7   FMaj7

Different voicings of the same chord are called *inversions*.

As long as you play with good rhythm, you can play as many voicings of the diminished 7 substitution as you like in place of the original dominant 7 chord.

Although it is a little dated, this is the first chord substitution that many jazz musicians learn as it gives instant access to an altered dominant sound.

The diminished 7 chord can be a little difficult to finger at first. One tip for the voicings on the 5th and 6th strings is to develop your finger dexterity by first fretting a dominant 7 chord and then quickly altering it to the dim 7 fingering. For example, try moving between the following fingerings:

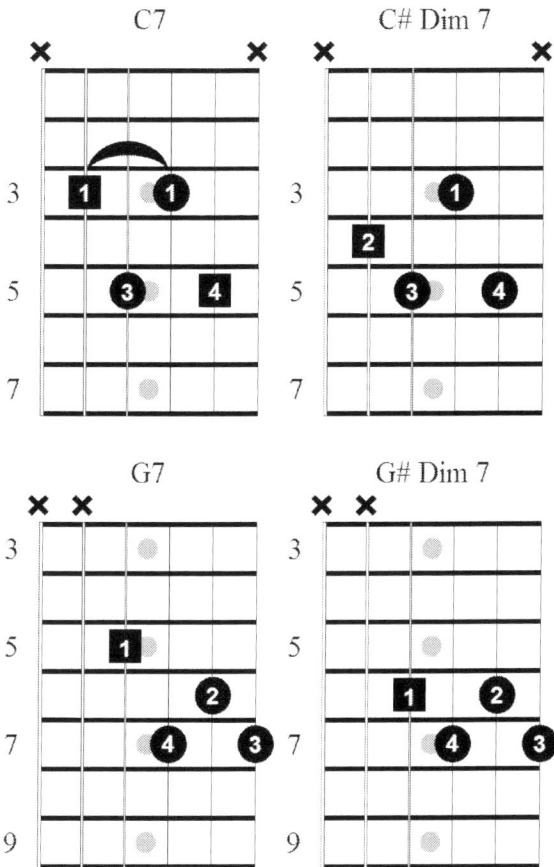

I would recommend fretting the 6th-string dim 7 chord with the following fingering:

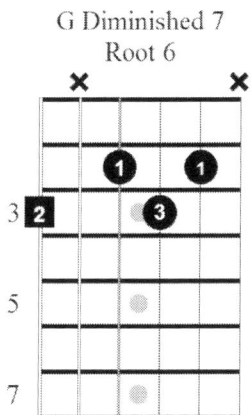

One common use of the diminished 7 chord is in bar six of a jazz blues:

Example 9f:

| Bb7 | Eb7 | Bb7 | Bm7 | E9 |

| Eb7 | E Dim7 | Bb7 | G7 |

| Cm7 | F7 | Bb7　G7 | Cm7 | F7 |

Using the E Dim 7 chord in bar six has the effect of creating an Eb7b9 chord which adds some tension before resolving back to the Bb root of the progression.

Try using a diminished substitution for each of the dominant 7 chords in the final two bars of the progression.

Instead of

| Bb7 | G7 | Cm7 | F7 |

Play a dim 7 chord on the 3rd (or b9) of each 7 chord:

| Bb7 | B Dim7 (G# Dim7) | Cm7 | A Dim7 (F# Dim7) |

Practice this diminished substitution with voicings based off the 6th, 5th and 4th strings.

Remember the following rule: "Any functional dominant chord can be replaced with a diminished chord built on the 3rd to create a 7b9 sound."

Chapter Ten: Major and Minor 6 Chords

Major and minor 6 chords are used frequently in many types of music, especially in early-era jazz. They are extremely useful to know.

Major 6 chords have the formula 1 3 5 6.

Minor 6 chords have the formula 1 b3 5 6.

In modal contexts you may occasionally need to play a b6 on a minor chord although that is fairly uncommon.

Major 6 chords

There are two ways to think about major 6 chords, either as the triad (1 3 5) with the added 6 or as a major7 chord where the 7th has been lowered by a tone. Both approaches are useful.

Major 6 chords are often seen notated as simply '6' or 'M6' for example C6 or CM6 although the former would be more common.

You can play major 6 chords with roots on the 6th, 5th and 4th strings in the following ways:

Example 10a:

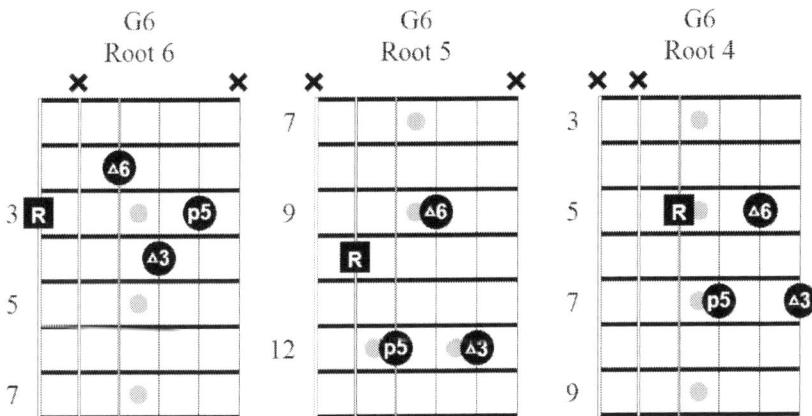

Examine the following diagrams and you will see why a major 6 chord can be thought of as a major 7th with the 7th lowered by a tone:

Example 10b:

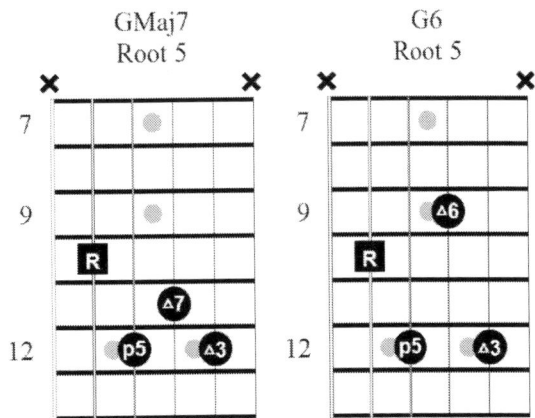

Major 6 chords are fairly bright-sounding and are normally used as a direct substitution for a major or major 7-type chord.

For example, in the chord sequence

Example 10c:

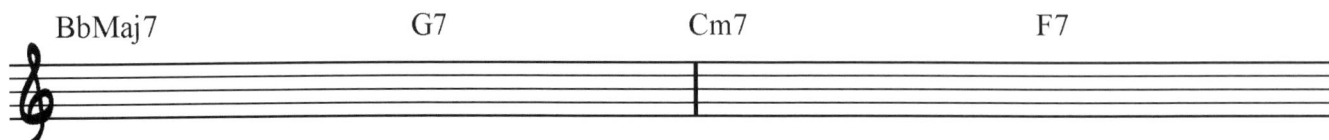

you could certainly play the following.

Example 10d:

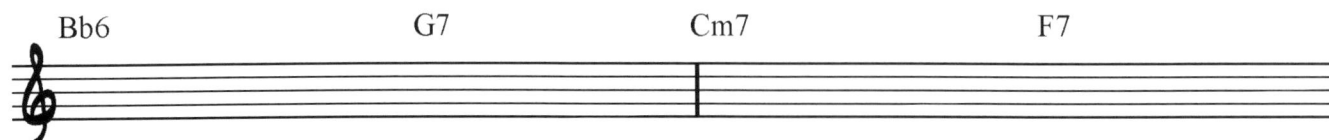

Although many older chord charts state major 6, a more modern approach would be to replace the major 6 chord with a major 7th.

Play through the following chord progression beginning from the 6th, 5th and 4th strings

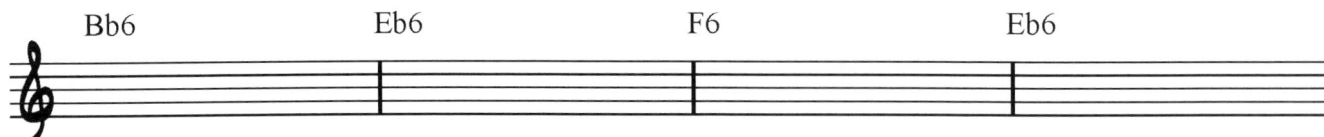

Substitutions for the Major 6 Chord

Study the notes in the chord of C6

1 3 5 6 = C E G A

C6

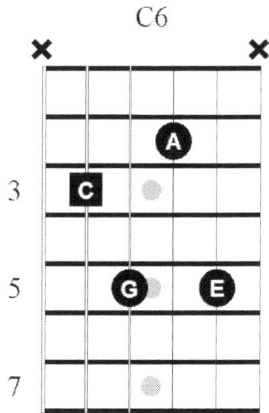

If we rearrange the order of the notes to

A C E G

Can you see that we have perfectly spelled out an A Minor 7 chord? With a root of A, the notes A C E G give us the formula 1 b3 5 b7.

We can use an A minor 7 chord as a direct substitution for a C6 chord.

To put this in more general terms: "To create a major 6 sound we can play a minor 7 chord based off the 6th of the original chord".

With substitutions like this it is important to use a fairly high register voicing of the substitution otherwise there is a danger of the substitution not being heard in the desired way. If the root of the substitution is too low, the listener might hear it as the true root of the chord when in fact it is an extension.

For example, if the bass player is playing a C bass note or figure we can use an Am7 voicing to make the listener hear a C6 chord.

Here are two voicings of Am7, one low and one high:

Example 10e:

The second voicing sounds much better because it is in a higher register, even though it contains the same notes. A general rule is that you want extensions i.e., the 6th to be in an 'upper' voice so the listener hears them as intended.

When I am using substitutions in this way I often aim to play them on just the top four strings, or at least voice them on the top half of the guitar neck when playing chords with the root on the 5th string. Experimentation is the key here so trust your own ears.

In Part Two of this book we will be learning many inversions of common chords, so you will have many ways to voice any chord structure. With this information it will be easy to *always* use a higher register voicing of a substitution chord.

For now, test yourself by working out which minor 7th chord you can use as a substitution to create the following chords:

1) G6
2) Bb6
3) F6

Answers below.[1]

For practice, work through the following chord progression using both the root position '6' voicings from earlier and by substituting a m7 chord on the 6th degree of the maj6 chord.

Bb6 – Bb D F G

Eb6 – Eb G Bb C

G6 – G B D E

D6 – D F# A B

---

[1] 1) Em7, 2) Gm7, 3) Dm7

1)

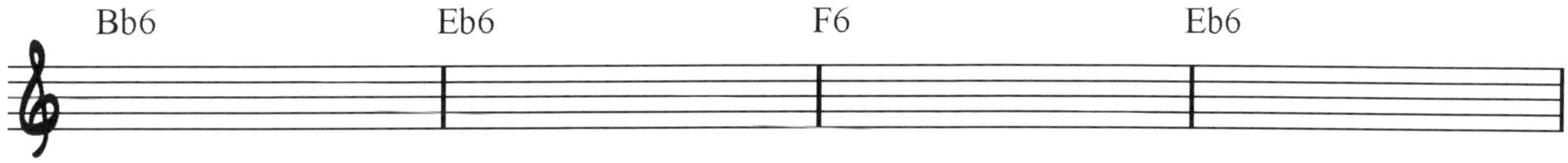
Bb6
Eb6
F6
Eb6

2)

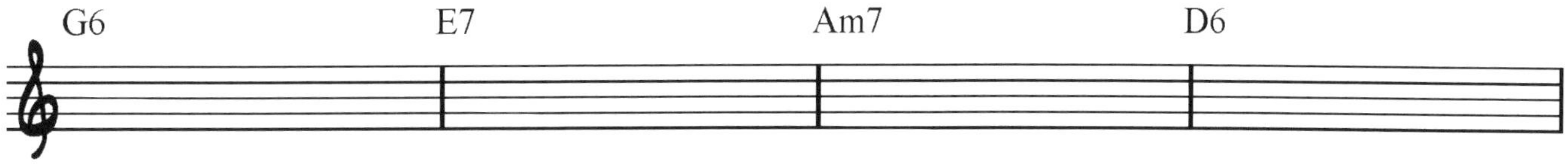
G6
E7
Am7
D6

Minor 6 Chords

Minor 6 chords have the formula 1 b3 5 6. They can be seen as a minor triad (1 b3 5) with an added 6, or as a minor 7 chord with the 7th lowered by a semitone. In the key of C the formula 1 b3 5 6 generates the notes C Eb G A.

Minor 6 chords are often used directly in place of m7 chords but sometimes the use of a m6 chord has some subtle implications when soloing.

Minor 6 chords can be voiced from the 6th, 5th and 4th strings in the following ways.

(Key of G)

Example 10f:

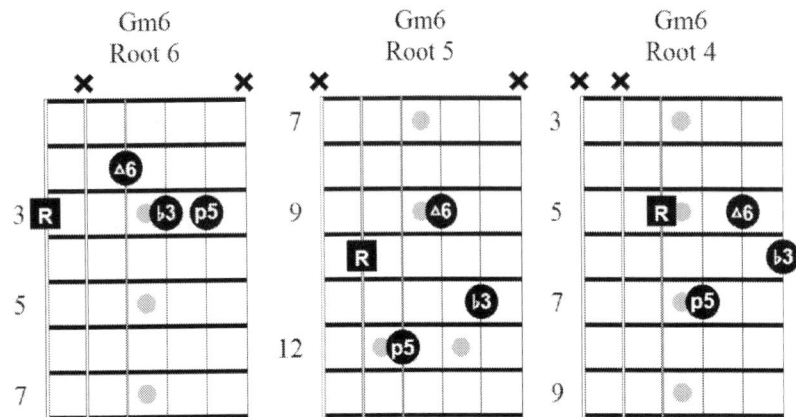

The following diagram shows that a m6 chord can be seen as a m7 chord with the b7 lowered by a semitone:

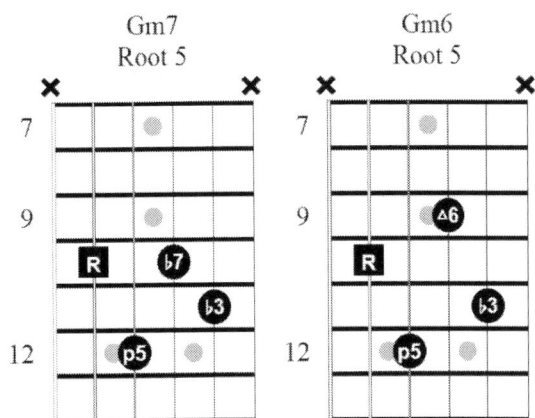

The following progression is one of the most common in which a minor 6 chord is used. Notice the minor/Major7 chord which you will learn more about in chapter twelve.

Example 10g:

Gm   Gm(Maj)7   Gm7   Gm6

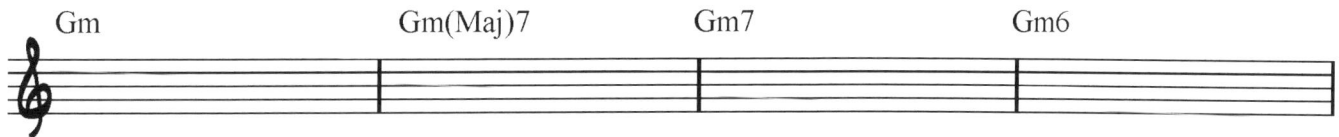

This sequence can be played:

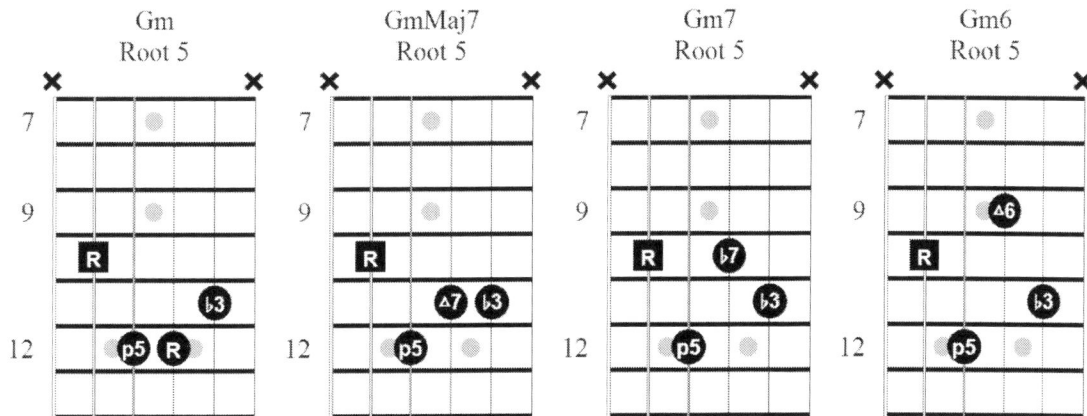

As you can see, the root of the chord descends by a semitone with each chord change.

If you see a m6 chord on a chord chart it is normally there for a specific reason, either the melody note of the tune is a 6th, or more likely the chart is telling you that this chord is the tonic chord in a *melodic minor* progression.

Without wading too deeply into music theory, the tonic (I) chord of a melodic minor scale harmonises to become a minMaj7 (pronounced "Minor Major 7th") chord. It is a *minor* chord with a *major* 7th and has the formula 1 b3 5 7. This is somewhat of a 'tense' chord and not really as stable a sound as you might look for in a 'home' chord.

Minor/Major 7ths are great chords, but they do have a very particular flavour which is not always appropriate for a minor ballad as you heard in the previous example. Often, a composer's solution is to replace the tonic mMaj7 with a m6. (Although for a great use of a mMaj7 chord as a tonic, check out Miles Davis' version of Solar)

If you're soloing and you see a m6 chord, a good first choice scale is often melodic minor.

Substitutions for the Minor 6 Chord

Just as we could substitute a m7 chord built on the 6th of the major 6 chord, we can do a similar thing for the minor 6 chord.

Look at the notes in the following diagram:

Cm6

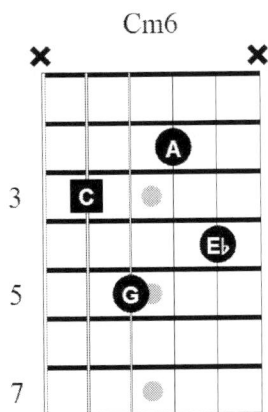

If you rearrange the notes to

A C Eb G,

you can see that you have perfectly spelled out an Am7b5 chord. With a root of A, the notes A C Eb G give us the formula 1 b3 b5 b7.

This means that a m7b5 chord played a 6th above the root creates a m6 chord.

To transfer this concept to other keys, simply count up a major 6th from the root and play a m7b5 chord on that note.

For example, to create a Gm6 chord, you would play an Em7b5 over a G bass note.

To create a Bm7 chord you would play a G#m7b5 chord over a B bass note.

On which note would you substitute a m7b5 chord to form the following m7 chords? Answers below.[2]

1) Dm6
2) Am6
3) F#m6

One of the nice things about the guitar is that it can be a very visual instrument. If you know what a major 6th interval looks like on the guitar you can always quickly find the correct substitution.

The major 6th interval will always look like this with a 6th string root:

---

[2] 1) Bm7b5, 2) F#m7b5, 3) Dm7b5

Major 6th
Interval

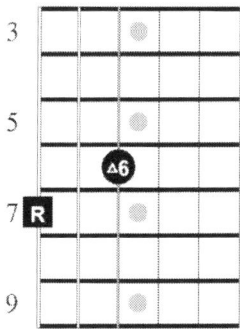

We know from chapter two that we can play a m7b5 chord with a root on the 4th string in the following way:

m7b5 Chord
4th String Root

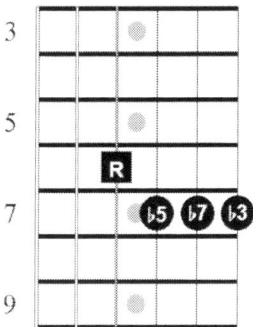

By combining these two diagrams we can show that one good way to visualise the m6 chord is

m6 Substitution
Shape

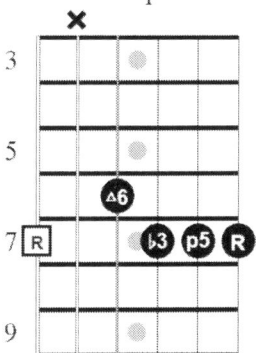

All you need to do is visualise the notes on the highest three strings on the same fret as the root of the 6th chord.

The same method works for forming a major 6 chord with a m7 chord:

Major 6 Substitution
Shape

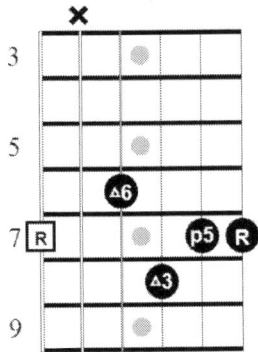

These visualisations are a good starting point when learning these chord substitutions, but with practice you will quickly learn to instantly apply important substitutions effortlessly and instantly.

We will learn much, much more about substitutions in Part Two of this book, but for now try to find as many different ways as you can to voice these important 6th chord substitutions.

Chapter Eleven: Major and Minor 6/9 chords

Major 6/9 chords can be a slightly ambiguous sound as they contain two extensions and no defining 7th degree. Also, when voiced on the guitar, the 3rd is quite often omitted.

The formula for a 'true' Major 6/9 chord is 1 3 5 6 9 although the chord tones that are included will often depend on finding a convenient fingering on the guitar.

Major 6/9 chords are often used as the final chord in a jazz tune to create a particular 'ending' sound that you will have heard in numerous outros. They are often used as a direct substitution for any major or major 7-type chord because they add richness and colour to the progression.

In the key of C, the formula 1 3 5 6 9 generates the following series of notes:

C E G A D

You will virtually always want to voice the 6 and 9 extensions in a higher octave than the root.

As a true major 6/9 voicing is a five-note chord, at least one note will normally be omitted on the guitar. These major 6/9 chords are often played as rootless voicings that omit the 3rd. While omitting the 3rd may seem to be 'against the rules', the human ear is very good at filling in the gaps, especially when these kinds of chords are played in the correct diatonic context.

We will look at some unique features of 6/9 chords that omit the 3rd later in this chapter, but for now learn these basic voicings of the major 6/9 chord in the key of G:

Example 11a:

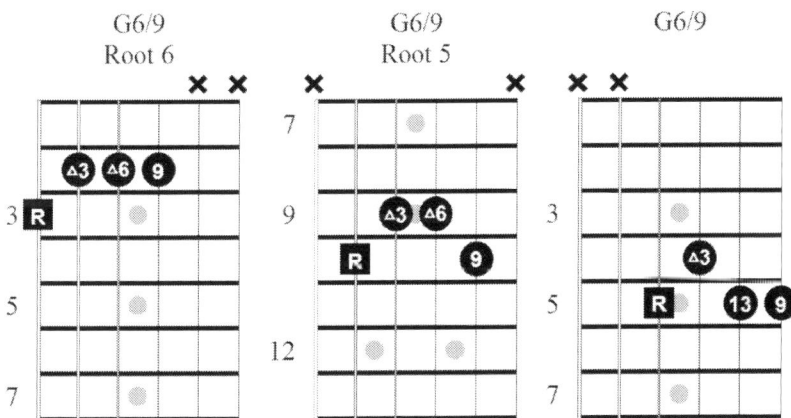

The next set of diagrams show how you can voice minor 6/9 chords:

Example 11b:

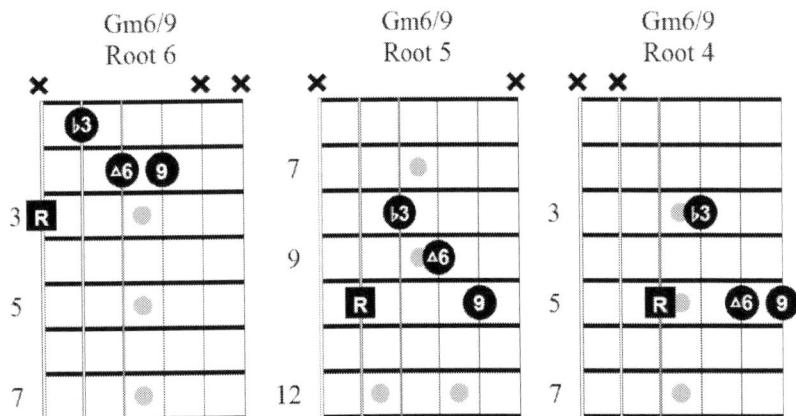

Minor 6/9 chords make great substitutions for any ii chord in a progression. In the following ii V I sequence in F Major, I have used a minor 6/9 chord for the ii chord, and a major 6/9 chord for the I chord.

Example 11c:

Try playing through the same sequence in different areas of the neck and exploring as many ways to use these voicings as possible.

There are some great tricks you can use when voicing 6/9 chords with no 3rd.

In the following diagram, the 6/9 chord is voiced on the top four strings of the guitar and this voicing does *not* include a 3rd. You should learn this shape as it is a very common guitar voicing. The root of the chord is marked in for your reference – it is optional.

Example 11d:

A 6/9
(No 3rd)

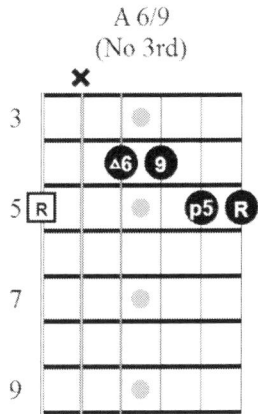

One interesting feature of 6/9 chords is that you can move the root up a 4th (across a string) and create another 6/9 chord with a different voicing:

D 6/9

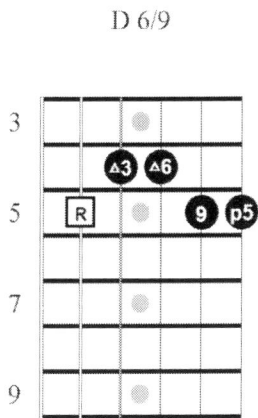

Try playing through the following chord progression:

Example 11e:

Due to this feature, you can get two voicings out of the same shape simply by sliding the 6/9 chord structure up and down. For example, the chord A6/9 can be played as

Example 11f:

In fact, this idea is used as a common ending. Listen to and learn the following common jazz ending. Notice how I use the open A string to provide a bass note to the final two 6/9 voicings:

Example 11g:

As shown in example 11b, 6/9 chords can be used as both a major I and major IV chord. They can also be used as a dominant chord voicing which would imply a '13' sound, however as they do not contain a b7 degree they are not usually a common voicing.

If you use6/9 chord voicings that does not include the 3rd, they also make excellent *Dorian* chords.

Sometimes in music a chord can simply be written to give the rhythm player freedom to use their own interpretation of a specific tonality. You may see written over a long, static chord progression something like "C Dorian" or "C Lydian". The composer wants you to use voicings and extensions that imply a particular modality. For "C Dorian" you would want to emphasise the b7 9 11 and 13th extensions. For "C Lydian" you would wish to use voicings that accentuate the #11.

The formula for the Dorian mode is 1 2 b3 4 5 6 b7, so the above 6/9 voicing with the formula 1 5 6 9 can be used to imply the extensions of a minor 6/9 chord with no b3. For this reason, it is a useful tonic voicing for both the harmonised major and the harmonised Dorian scale. As the Dorian mode is built on the second degree of the major scale, the 1 5 6 9 voicing works as a harmonisation of chord ii.

If you wished, you could play the first four chords of the jazz standard Autumn Leaves in the following way:

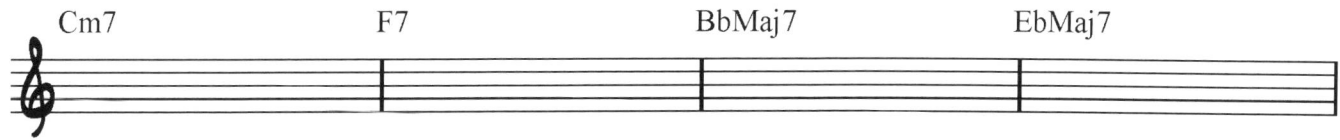

Cm7   F7   BbMaj7   EbMaj7

Example 11h:

C6/9
(Cm7)

F6/9
(F13)

Bb6/9
(Bbmaj7)

Eb6/9
(EbMaj7)

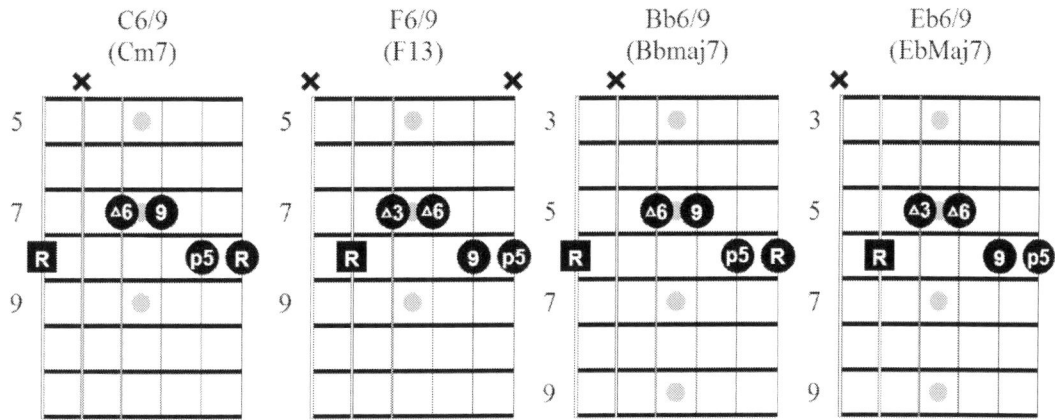

6/9 chords are very versatile chords that can be used in a wide variety of different contexts.

Chapter Twelve: Minor/Major7 Chords

The m(Maj7) chord occurs naturally in music when you harmonise the tonic chords of both the harmonic and the melodic minor scales. It has the formula 1 b3 5 7 and in the key of C this generates the notes C Eb G B.

Harmonic Minor = 1 2 b3 4 5 b6 7

Melodic Minor = 1 2 b3 4 5 6 7

As discussed in the section on minor 6 chords, composers often avoid using the m(Maj7) chord as a tonic resolution point due to the unstable nature of this chord.

Useful guide tone voicings for this chord include the following.

Example 12a:

They can be played in the following ways as full 1 b3 5 7 chords.

Example 12b:

These chords are rarely used anywhere other than as a tonic chord in a progression that is derived from either the harmonic or melodic minor scales.

We have already looked at one common progression that uses the m(Maj7) chord:

Gm	Gm7	GmMaj7	Gm6

In the above progression, the tonic note (G) can be heard descending by a semitone as you move through the voicings.

To recap, you can play the above progression in the following way:

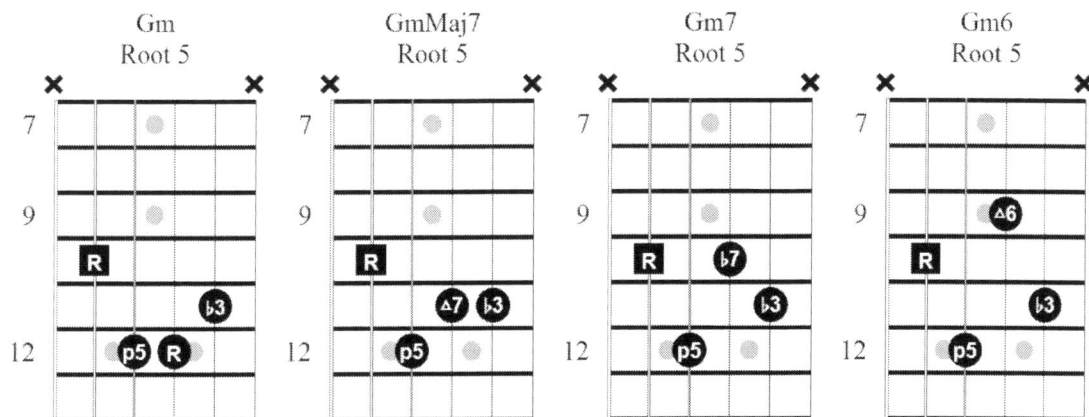

Gm — Root 5   GmMaj7 — Root 5   Gm7 — Root 5   Gm6 — Root 5

Minor(Maj7) chords crop up fairly commonly in minor-key jazz tunes such as My Funny Valentine and Solar.

Chapter Thirteen: Major 7b5 and Major 7#5 Chords

The Maj7b5 Chord

As we learnt in chapter seven with Maj7-type chords, some care must be taken when naming b5 and #11 intervals which are often used interchangeably, although this is theoretically incorrect. Maj7b5 implies that the natural 5th has been replaced with the b5, whereas maj7#11 implies that there could be a natural 5th and a #11 in the chord, although this is not common practice with guitar voicings.

This means that a Maj7b5 chord technically contains the intervals

1 3 b5 7.

A Maj7#11 chord *could* contain the intervals 1 3 5 7 and #11.

The larger voicing is possible on the piano where there is the facility to spread the notes in a dense chord far apart, but on the guitar this is not always an option for us. Generally guitarists will normally omit the 5th in a Maj7#11 chord so it becomes interchangeable with a Maj7b5 chord.

The Maj7#11 chord is formed naturally when we harmonise the 4th degree of the major scale. It is the definitive 'Lydian chord'.

Here are three common voicings.

Example 13a:

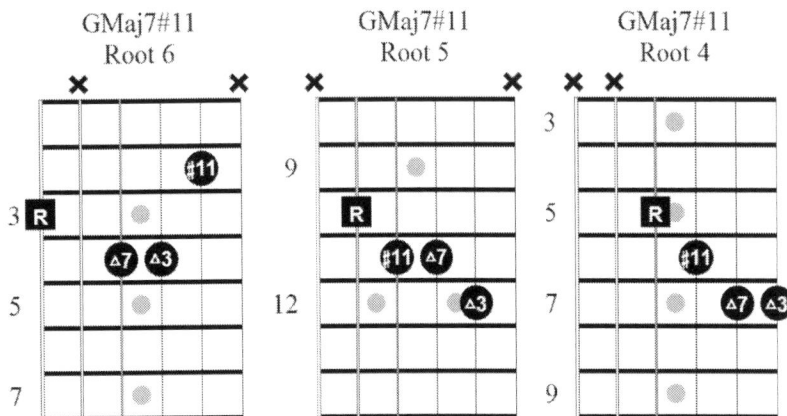

As you may expect, this chord can be used directly in place of the IV chord in a major progression.

Example 13b:

It is sometimes also used in place of the tonic chord in jazz endings.

Example 13c:

Try using the Maj7#11 chord as both a substitute for the IV chord in a major progression and as a 'colourful' I chord.

The Maj7#5 Chord

The Maj7#5 chord occurs naturally in both the harmonised melodic minor and harmonic minor scales. It is formed when you build a chord on the b3rd degree of either scale.

The formula for a Maj7#5 chord is 1 3 #5 7.

From a root of C this generates the notes C E G# B.

Unlike the Maj7#11 chord there is no ambiguity here regarding #11s and b5s. You will never play a natural 5th and a #5th in the same chord.

Despite being a 'legitimate' chord built from a scale degree of common scales, the Maj#5 isn't a particularly common sound in music.

You can voice a Major7#5 chord in the following ways on the guitar.

Example 13d:

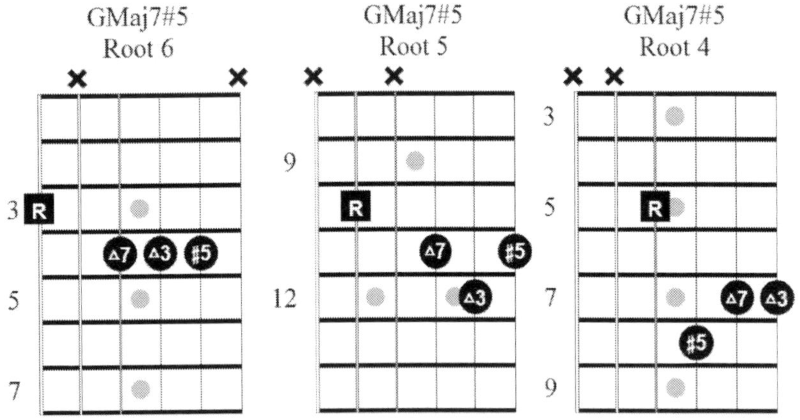

Maj7#5 chords are quite often played rootless because they can be viewed as a simple major triad played over a bass note.

For example, in a Maj7#5 chord in the key of G (above) we have the notes:

G B D# and F#

We can rearrange these notes to reveal a B major triad (B, D# and F#) which when played over the G root create a Maj7#5 chord.

This can be seen more easily in the following diagrams.

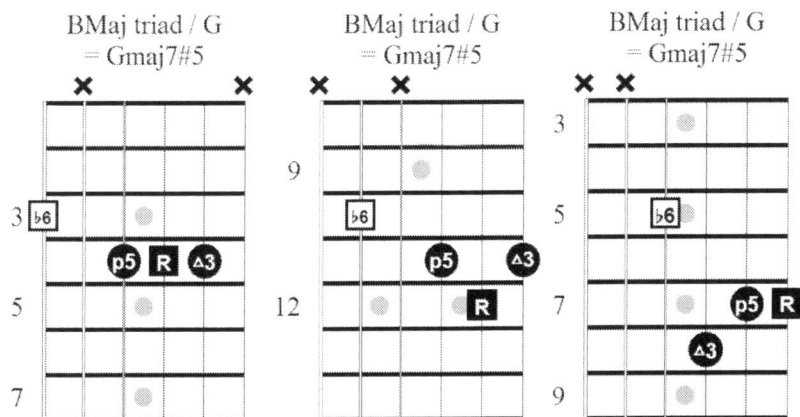

BMaj triad / G = Gmaj7#5 — BMaj triad / G = Gmaj7#5 — BMaj triad / G = Gmaj7#5

One name for this kind of 'triad-over-a-bass-note' voicing is a 'slash chord' because it can be defined as an X Triad / Y Bass note.

In this case, the chord 'GMaj7#5' can be seen as 'B Major / G'.

To form a Maj7#5 sound we can play a major triad one major third above the root.

To form a CMaj7#5 sound we can play an E Major Triad over C.

How would you use a slash chord voicing to form the following chords?

1) DMaj7#5
2) EMaj7#5
3) BMaj7#5

Answers at the bottom of the page.[3]

Slash chords can be a tricky concept to put into practice at first. Begin by learning the 1 3 5 major triad shapes in the previous diagrams and then learn to quickly place them on the major 3rd of the desired root note.

[3] 1) F# Major / D 2) G# Major / E 3) D# Major / B

Using Maj7#5 Chords

The most common use of a Maj7#5 chord is an altered home chord. The following progressions show two typical examples of it in context.

Example 13e:

Example 13f:

Chapter Fourteen: Building Extended Chords with Diatonic Substitutions

Until this point in the book we have generally been selecting specific intervals to form particular types of chords. In this chapter we will look in more depth at the idea of diatonic substitutions. We will go into much more detail in Part Two of this series, but for now it is important that you understand some essential concepts before moving forward.

A 'diatonic' substitution is one where the *substitute chord* originates from the *same key* or harmonised scale as the *original chord*.

The most common use of this principle is to build chords with natural extensions by continually 'stacking' intervals above a bass note.

For example, let's take the scale of C Major:

C	D	E	F	G	A	B	C	D	E	F	G	A	B	C
(1)	2	(3)	4	(5)	6	(7)	1	(9)	3	(11)	5	(13)	7	1

We know we can build a CMaj7 chord in the following way:

1 3 5 7 (C E G B)

A CMaj9 chord that contains *every note* is formed with

1 3 5 7 9 (C E G B D).

A CMaj11 chord is formed with

1 3 5 7 9 11 (C E G B D F).

And a CMaj13 chord is formed with

1 3 5 7 9 11 13 (C E G B D F A).

As previously discussed, we do not normally wish to include every note in these extended chords so we often discard less important intervals like the 5th and the root when constructing them.

Another way to reach the higher extensions of a chord is to use a substitution. By building a new 7th chord from one of the chord tones of the original chord we can reach the 'upper structures' (extensions) easily and use chord forms we already know to imply a richer, extended chord sound.

Look at the notes in CMaj9; C E G B D.

If we get rid of the root (C), we are left with the notes E G B D. These notes form an Em7 chord.

By playing an Em7 chord over a bass note of C we have created a CMaj9 sound.

The following example shows this concept played on the guitar. The root (C) is included just for your reference. The Em7 chord is shown in black dots and the intervals as they relate to the root note of C are given.

Example 14a:

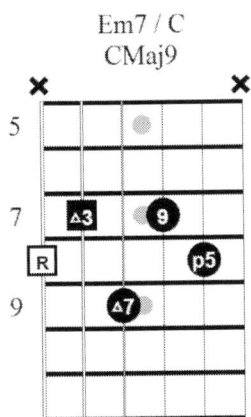

Em7 / C
CMaj9

By simply using an Em7 chord in place of a CMaj7 chord we have created a CMaj9 sound. The note C is not played in this voicing which is often desirable as other instruments, such as the bass, will normally be playing it.

The rule is that we can always play a m7 chord on the 3rd of a Maj7 chord to create a Maj9th chord.

In fact, we can use a '7th' chord built on the 3rd of any other 7th chord to extend it up to the 9th.

If we know the harmonised major scale, we can always simply jump a 3rd to find out which 7th chord to use as a substitution. Here is the harmonised scale of C Major.

I	ii	iii	IV	V	vi	vii
CMaj7	Dm7	Em7	FMaj7	G7	Am7	Bm7b5

In the previous example, we used chord iii (Em7) as a substitution to form a CMaj9 chord.

Interval from C	1	3	5	7	9
CMaj7	C	E	G	B	
Em7		E	G	B	D

Now, let's form a Dm9 chord in the same way.

Interval from D	1	b3	5	7	9
Dm7	D	F	A	C	
FMaj7		F	A	C	E

This can be viewed on the guitar in the following manner:

Example 14b:

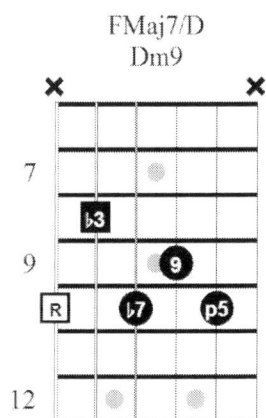

By building a Maj7 chord on the b3rd of a minor 7 chord, we create a rootless m9 chord.

The same process can be used to build a dominant 9 chord.

To form a dominant 9 chord, we can play a m7b5 chord of the 3rd of a dominant 7 chord.

Putting this into the key of C, we can use the Bm7b5 chord to imply a rootless G9 sound.

Interval from G	1	3	5	b7	9
G7	G	B	D	F	
Bm7b5		B	D	F	A

On the guitar this looks like:

Example 14c:

Bm7b5/G
G9

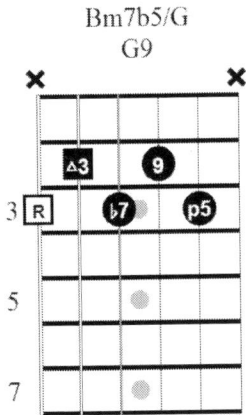

Finally, to create a m7b5b9 sound, we can play a m7 chord on the b3 of the original m7b5 chord.

In the key of C this would mean playing a Dm7 chord over Bm7b5.

Interval from B	1	b3	b5	b7	b9
Bm7b5	B	D	F	A	
Dm7		D	F	A	C

Example 14d:

Dm7/B
Bm7b5b9

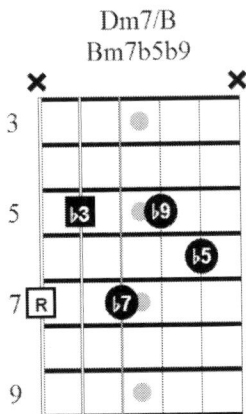

Every substitute chord in this context is taken from the harmonised major scale. When each of the degrees of the major scale are harmonised we generate the following sequence of chords.

This may seem like a lot of rules, but because these examples derive from the harmonised major scale (which always harmonises in the same way) these rules are constant. In other words, to form a Maj9 sound, you can *always* play a m7th on the 3rd.

Here is a summary of the last few pages:

Original Chord Type	Substitution on the 3rd	Rootless Extended Chord
Maj7	m7	Maj9
m7	Maj7	m9
7	m7b5	9
m7b5	m7	m7b5b9

To test yourself, work out which chord could you build on the 3rd of the following chords to form a '9th' voicing.[4]

1) FMaj7
2) EMaj7
3) Gm7
4) Bbm7
5) F7
6) A7
7) Gm7b5
8) Dm7b5

If we want to reach higher extensions we can simply build 7th chords from the 5th or even the 7th of the original chord. It is important to remember that as the substitute chord gets further away from the root of the original, we are replacing more chord tones with extensions and so the original tonality can be harder to hear.

Take a look again at the harmonised C major scale.

I	ii	iii	IV	V	vi	vii
CMaj7	Dm7	Em7	FMaj7	G7	Am7	Bm7b5

To build a CMaj11 chord we can play a G7 chord on the 5th of CMaj7.

Interval from C	1	3	5	7	9	11
CMaj7	C	E	G	B		
G7			G	B	D	F

---

[4] 1) Am7, 2) G#m7, 3) BMaj7, 4) Dbmaj7, 5) Am7b5, 6) C#m7b5, 7) Bbm7, 8) Fm7

Example 14e:

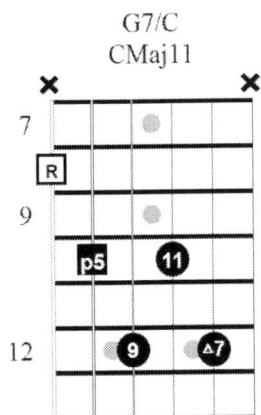

Played over a bass note of C, the chord G7 gives us the chord tones 5, 7, 9 and 11.

You will notice that the defining major 3rd is now omitted (although in the case of a CMaj11 chord this is possibly desirable due to the clash between the 3rd and the 11th).

When we use these kinds of substitutions on the 5th and 7th of a chord, we include more extensions but less of the original chord tones.

In Part Two of this series we will learn how to voice the most important chord structures in many different inversions, all over the neck. This is often the best time to start applying upper structure substitutions as we can easily control the range and pitch of the added extensions.

Another concern is the range in which the substitution is played. It is always going to be better to play these substitutions on string groups 1 to 4, 2 to 5 or even just higher up on the neck where the extensions will not clash with chord tones played by other instruments.

There are many different instrumental line-ups, ranging from solo guitar right through to big bands and using chord substitutions in this way can often depend on the density of the harmony and the parts played by other instruments.

Bearing all this in mind, let's continue our look at building 7th chords on the 5th of each original chord type.

Remember that all the substitutions we are using are diatonic to the harmonised major scale. By simply counting up five notes from the root of the chord and looking at the following chart, we can easily see the substitution we need to use to create an 11th chord.

I	ii	iii	IV	V	vi	vii
CMaj7	Dm7	Em7	FMaj7	G7	Am7	Bm7b5

To form a Dm11 chord we can play an Am7 chord on the 5th.

Interval from D	1	b3	5	7	9	11
Dm7	D	F	A	C		
Am7			A	C	E	G

Example 14f:

Am7/D
Dm11

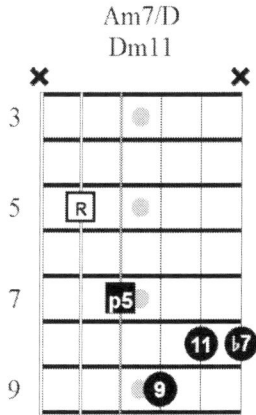

To form a G11 chord we can play a Dm7 chord on the 5th.

Interval from G	1	3	5	b7	9	11
G7	G	B	D	F		
Bm7b5			D	F	A	C

Example 14g:

Dm/G
G11

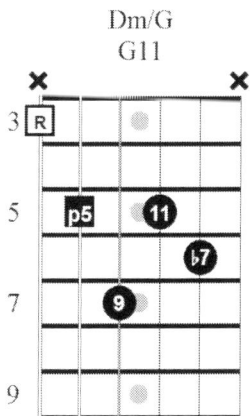

Finally, we can play a FMaj7 chord on the 5th of Bm7b5 to create a Bm11b5b9 chord:

Interval from B	1	b3	b5	b7	b9	11
Bm7b5	B	D	F	A		
FMaj7			F	A	C	E

Example 14h:

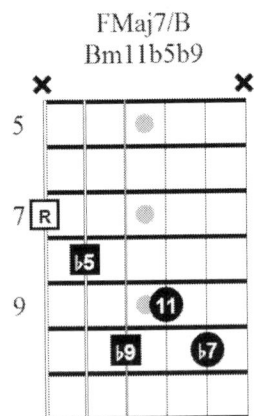

FMaj7/B
Bm11b5b9

To summarise 7th chord substitutions on the 5th you can use the following table.

Original Chord Type	Substitution on the 5th	Rootless Extended Chord
Maj7	7	Maj11
m7	m7	m11
7	m7	11
m7b5	Maj7	m11b5b9

Finally, before we look at some uses of these types of chords, I will summarise the extensions that are created when we use 7th chords built on the 7th of each chord.

Original Chord Type	Substitution on the 7th	Rootless Extended Chord
Maj7	m7b5	Maj13
m7	Maj7	m13
7	Maj7	13
m7b5	m7	m13b5b9

Great care must be taken with these substitutions built on the 7th as now the substituted chord has only one note in common with the original chord.

Using Diatonic Substitutions

As you might imagine, diatonic substitutions built on the 5th and the 7th are a lot less common than substitutions built on the 3rd.

When we build a 7th substitution from the 3rd we're only losing the root and replacing it with a 9th. As you've heard throughout this book, the 9th is a very acceptable extension and can be used almost anywhere.

Try playing through the following progression using backing track one.

Example 14i:

Cm7	F7	BbMaj7	

This time, build a 9th chord on the Cm7 chord by using a substitution on the b3.

The notes of Cm7 are C Eb G Bb

So you can use chord EbMaj7 to create a Cm9 sound.

Play the progression again over backing track one, but this time substitute EbMaj7 for the Cm7 chord.

Example 14j:

EbMaj7 (Cm9)	F7	BbMaj7	

Repeat the exercise, but this time use the substitution on the F7 chord. To create a '9' sound we play a m7b5 chord on the 3rd.

Example 14k:

Cm7	Am7b5 (F9)	BbMaj7	

Finally, repeat the process but this time build a BbMaj9th. To create a Maj9 sound we can play a m7 chord on the 3rd.

Example 14l:

Cm7	F7	Dm7 (BbMaj9)

(empty staff)

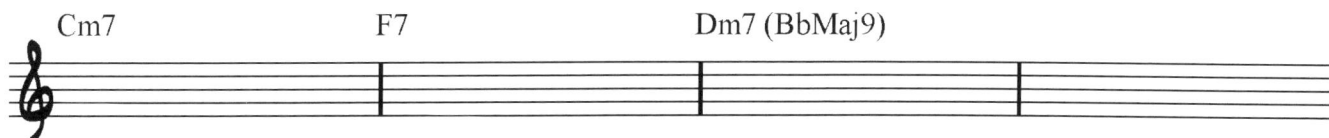

As we are playing these substitutions with a strong bassline on the backing track, it is easy to hear how the substitution functions to build a 9th on each chord.

If you have a strong rhythm section or backing track you can normally add in as many 9th substitutions as you like. Try combining the three substitutions above:

Example 14m:

EbMaj7 (Cm9)	Am7b5 (F9)	Dm7 (BbMaj9)

(empty staff)

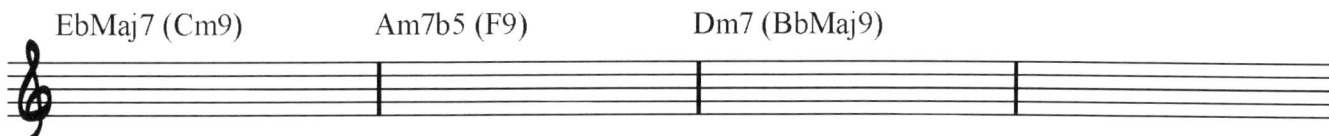

Try this with and without the backing track and notice how the context of the chords changes.

Using this system to build chords on the 5th or 7th to access the higher extensions of the chord, it is normally useful to have a strong sense of key. These kinds of voicings are often used over static chord vamps where there is not much harmonic movement. Even then, they need to be played with good rhythm and placement.

Over an eight bar vamp of D Minor 7, we can easily begin to use upper structure substitutions to add interest and movement to the static harmony.

The 7th chords built on the b3 5 and b7 of D minor are

Interval from D	1	b3	5	7	9	11	13
Dm7	D	F	A	C			
FMaj7		F	A	C	E		
Am7			A	C	E	G	
Cmaj7				C	E	G	B

Backing track two is a Dm7 vamp.

Practice superimposing the chords of CMaj7, Am7 and FMaj7 over this vamp. Return to Dm7 every now and then to resolve your chord line. Play all the substitution chords with a root either on the 5th string or the 4th string to keep the extensions from clashing with the rhythm guitar part.

Example 14n:

Going forward, it is important that you understand these types of substitutions although they really are just the tip of the iceberg. Experimentation is the best way to internalise them but don't get too complex too soon. The concept of building a 7th chord from the 3rd of an original chord is an important one so make sure you have memorised and can apply these voicings in all keys.

Here are the most important ones to learn for now, just to refresh your memory.

Original Chord Type	Substitution on the 3rd	Rootless Extended Chord
Maj7	m7	Maj9
m7	Maj7	m9
7	m7b5	9
m7b5	m7	m7b5b9

Very soon, you will stop having to think about these formulas because the chord shapes will become second nature and magically appear on the guitar neck in front of you. The ultimate goal is to be able to see the fretboard simply as intervals from any root note. This happens much faster than you would expect, especially when working with these kinds of substitutions.

Practice over static chord vamps, for example, practice playing voicings of F#m7b5 over a 32 bar vamp of D7 to create a D9 sound. Keep it simple and work on one chord type at a time. Remember that once you know the patterns, these substitutions work in the same way in every key and the secret to making them work is to use high register chord voicings.

Conclusions and Introduction to Part Two

Part One of this series has covered a great deal of harmonic material, from the basics of how common chords are formed right through to some important substitution concepts.

What I want you to take from Part One (apart from a vastly improved chord vocabulary!) is the conceptual information contained here.

You have learned how to form, play and apply every common chord structure in contemporary music and I hope that if something comes up that you've not seen before, you can return to first principles in order to quickly build a usable voicing. Remember, that if you're in doubt in a live situation you can always rely on playing just the correct triad if you don't have the full chord voicing already under your fingers. If it's *really* tough, it's OK to sit out for a bar. We've all done it!

Part One has focused on developing an excellent grounding in the basics. You have learnt a minimum of three root-position voicings of each chord discussed in the book. You can play these with roots on the 6th, 5th and 4th strings. These will get you through virtually any gig. Equally importantly, you now have an understanding of how chords are formed and which notes you can omit in complex structures.

The most important thing you can do now is to internalise this information. The quickest way to do that is simply to play. Get yourself a copy of The Real Book and start playing through some tunes. You will learn a lot about music very quickly. Experiment by changing chord qualities. If you see a m7 chord, try changing it to a m6, m9 or a m6/9. You will immediately learn to recognise when these substitutions can be applied.

About Part Two

In Part Two of the series, we look at getting more artistic and musical with how we choose to play the important chord structures introduced in this book. We will be taking an exhaustive look at advanced chord voicings, inversions and substitutions.

The way a chord is voiced on an instrument has a huge impact on its sound. In Part One, we learned that a 7th chord is built by stacking the root, 3rd, 5th and 7th degrees. The chord of CMaj7 can be written like this:

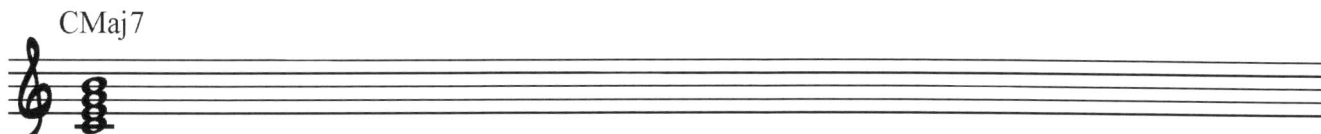

CMaj7

However, the notes do not have to be played in this order. The chord can be *inverted* so that a different note is in the bass.

By raising the bottom note (the root) of the chord by an octave, the lowest note (the 3rd) becomes the bass.

CMaj7

First Inversion

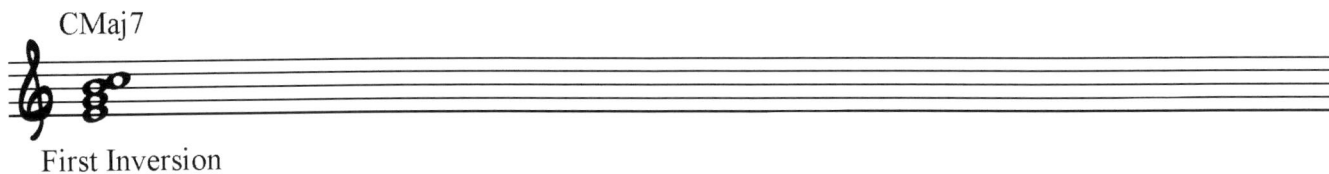

This chord voicing is still a CMaj7, but due to the different inversion of the notes, it has a different musical quality.

As there are four notes in the chord, it can be inverted four times (including the root position voicing):

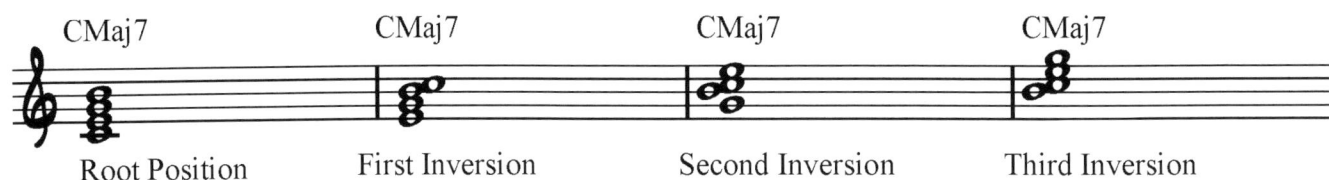

CMaj7   **CMaj7**   **CMaj7**   **CMaj7**

Root Position   *First Inversion*   *Second Inversion*   *Third Inversion*

Each of these inversions is a legitimate voicing of a CMaj7 chord and each has a subtly different flavour.

While the above voicings are not necessarily useful to play on the guitar, it is very important to know this principle of inversions because are some very useful and important ways to structure and voice every 7th chord by applying the concept of 'drop voicings'.

The most common chord structure played in jazz guitar is the 'drop 2' voicing. It is created by dropping the second highest note of the chord down by one octave. It is voiced like this:

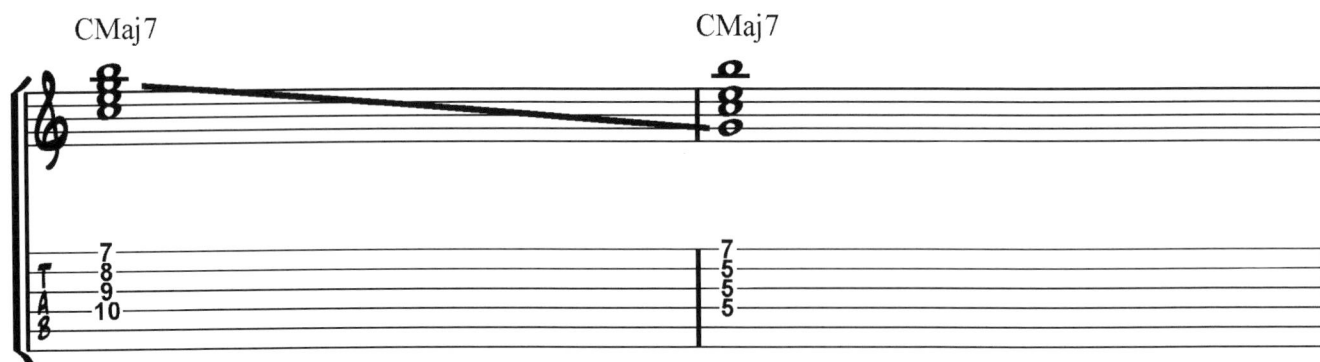

CMaj7   **CMaj7**

The second chord in the above diagram is a root position CMaj7 chord played as a drop 2 voicing.

There are four inversions of the root position CMaj7 chord and each one can be played as a drop 2 chord. Notice in the above example that this chord is voiced on just the top four strings of the guitar. These four-string chords can be transferred across to the 2nd-5th string and 3rd-6th string groups.

This gives a total of twelve chord shapes on the guitar to voice these drop 2 chords. Other chord types that will be taught are 'drop 3' voicings and 'drop 2 drop 4' voicings.

This may seem daunting, but if you've ever listened to jazz guitar chord melody players like Joe Pass, and wondered where all those beautiful chords come from, this kind of study is the best place to start investigating their mastery of the guitar.

There is a very useful, structured way to learn all these voicings which I will teach you in Part Two of this series. Not every chord type in every voicing is useful, and knowing which avenues to pursue and which to avoid will save you hours in the practice room.

The outcome of this type of study is that you will gain complete command over your fretboard and be able to voice beautiful, complex chords with ease and precision. I personally spent years learning jazz guitar soloing, but the thing that really helped me understand the fretboard was learning these amazing voicings.

Part Two also goes into much more detail about the practical application of chord substitutions. In Part One we covered the basics of diatonic chord substitution. This will be expanded upon and applied musically using the 'drop' voicings described above. Because we will have many more chord voicings to choose from, it is easy to create some beautiful, complex chords just by using the structures we already know. As always many recorded musical examples will be given.

In Part Two, we will also look at 'non-diatonic' substitutions. The idea once again is to use the 7th structures we already know to create chords with chromatic or 'altered' extensions. This technique is most commonly applied to functional dominant chords to add chromatic tensions as described in chapter seven and is similar to the diminished substitution ideas in chapter eight. By knowing how to substitute simple 7th voicings for dominant chords, it is easy to create rich, complex, altered dominant textures.

Part Two of Guitar Chords in Context teaches you how to advance your chord skills quickly, systematically and musically. It will truly open up the guitar neck for you.

Quick Chord Reference Guide

Chord Type	Construction	Notes Often Omitted On Guitar
Maj	1 3 5	
Min	1 b3 5	
Dim (mb5)	1 b3 b5	
Aug (Maj#5)	1 3 #5	
Maj7	1 3 5 7	
Min7	1 b3 5 b7	
7	1 3 5 b7	
m7b5	1 b3 b5 b7	
Dim7	1 b3 b5 bb7	
m(Maj7)	1 b3 5 7	
m(Maj9)	1 b3 5 7 9	5
Maj9	1 3 5 7 9	5

Chord Type	Construction	Notes Often Omitted On Guitar
m9	1 b3 5 7 9	5
9	1 3 5 b7 9	5
m7b9b5	1 b3 b5 b7 b9	1
m9b5	1 b3 b5 b7 9	1
Maj11	1 3 5 7 9 11	3, 9
Maj7sus4	1 5 7 11	
m11	1 b3 5 b7 9 11	1, 5, 9
11	1 3 5 b7 9 11	1, 5, 9
m11b9b5	1 b3 b5 b7 b9 11	1, b5, b9
Maj13	1 3 5 7 9 11 13	1, 9, 11
Maj13sus4	1 4 5 7 9 11 13	1, 5, 9, 11
m13	1 b3 5 b7 9 11 13	1, 5, 9, 11
13	1 3 5 b7 9 11 13	1, 11
7 alt	1 3 5 b7 + Any of b9 #9 b5(#11) #5(b13)	1, 5

Other Books from Fundamental Changes

Fundamental Changes in Jazz Guitar I: The Major ii V I for Bebop Guitar

Minor ii V Mastery for Jazz Guitar

Jazz Blues Soloing for Guitar

Guitar Scales in Context

Drop 2 Chord Voicings for Jazz and Modern Guitar

The CAGED System and 100 Licks for Blues Guitar

The Complete Guide to Playing Blues Guitar Book One: Rhythm Guitar

The Complete Guide to Playing Blues Guitar Book Two: Melodic Phrasing

The Complete Guide to Playing Blues Guitar Book Three: Beyond Pentatonics

The Complete Guide to Playing Blues Guitar Compilation (Paperback)

The Complete Technique, Theory and Scales Compilation for Guitar (Paperback)

Sight Reading Mastery for Guitar

Complete Technique for Modern Guitar

Rock Guitar Un-CAGED: The CAGED System and 100 Licks for Rock Guitar

Be Social

Join over 4000 people getting six free guitar lessons each day on Facebook:

www.facebook.com/FundamentalChangesInGuitar

Keep up to date on Twitter

@Guitar_Joseph

Cover Photo: ShutterStock Petr Malyshev

Printed in Germany
by Amazon Distribution
GmbH, Leipzig